Sue Hackman

7.99

Fast Forward Writing

LEVEL **4** to LEVEL **5**

Hodder Murray

A MEMBER OF THE HODDER HEADLINE GROUP

Acknowledgements

Acknowledgements for copyright text, artwork, photographs and images on page 138.

Orders: please contact Bookpoint Ltd, 130 Milton Park, Abingdon, Oxon OX14 4SB.
Telephone: (44) 01235 827720, Fax: (44) 01235 400454.
Lines are open from 9.00am – 6.00pm, Monday to Saturday, with a 24 hour message answering service.
You can also order through our website www.hoddereducation.co.uk

British Library Cataloguing in Publication Data
A catalogue record for this title is available from The British Library

ISBN-13: 0 340 81192 7
ISBN-13: 978 0 340 81192 4

First published 2004
Impression number   10 9 8 7 6 5 4 3 2
Year   2008 2007 2006 2005

Cover artwork by Neil Leslie, Début Art.
Typeset by Endangered Species, Essex.
Printed in Italy for Hodder Murray, an imprint of Hodder Education, a member of the Hodder Headline Group, 338 Euston Road, London NW1 3BH.

Contents

A. Sharpening your writing

Aims of this unit of work

- To make writing more concise
- To improve accuracy and precision
- To make points more articulate and well-argued

Objectives addressed (by year)

Year 7 objectives

Wd14	Word meaning in context
Wd20	Connectives
S9	Starting paragraphs
S10	Paragraph structure
S13e	Persuasion
Wr15	Express a view
Wr16	Validate an argument

Year 8 objectives

Wr2	Anticipate reader reaction
Wr6	Figurative language
Wr13	Present a case persuasively
Wr17	Integrate evidence

Year 9 objectives

Wr6	Creativity in non-literary texts
Wr10	Explain connections
Wr11	Descriptive detail
Wr13	Influence audience

B. Improving your writing process

Aims of this unit of work

- To improve the quality of planning
- To improve the quality of the drafting process
- To improve the quality of composition

Objectives addressed (by year)

Year 7 objectives

Wd20	Connectives
S12	Sequencing paragraphs
Wr1	Drafting process
Wr2	Planning formats
Wr3	Exploratory writing

Year 8 objectives

R1	Combine information
R3	Notemaking formats
R9	Influence of technology
Wr1	Effective planning
Wr2	Anticipate reader reaction
Wr10	Effective information

Year 9 objectives

Sn8	Connectives for developing thought
R2	Synthesise information
Wr1	Review own writing
Wr4	Presentational devices
Wr9	Integrate information
Wr12	Effective presentation of information

C. Improving your style

Aims of this unit of work

- To secure control of longer, more complex sentences
- To improve coherence and cohesion
- To enhance narrative control

Objectives addressed (by year)

Year 7 objectives

Wd20	Connectives
S1	Subordinate clauses
S2	Noun phrases
S3	Boundary punctuation
S8	Starting paragraphs
S10	Paragraph structure
R14	Language choices
Wr14	Evocative description

Year 8 objectives

Wd10	Prepositions and connectives
S1	Complex sentences
S3	Colons and semicolons
S6	Grouping sentences
S7	Cohesion and coherence
Wr10	Effective information

Year 9 objectives

Wd8	Connectives for developing thought
S1	Complex sentences
S2	Punctuation for clarity and effect
R12	Rhetorical devices
Wr10	Explain connections
Wr11	Descriptive detail

D. Improving your composition

Aims of this unit of work

- To expand the repertoire of non-fiction writing
- To deal with more complex subject matter and demands
- To make better use of rhetorical devices in non-fiction

Objectives addressed (by year)

Year 7 objectives

S13a	Information
S13c	Explanation
S134e	Persuasion
S13f	Discursive writing
Wr6	Characterisation
Wr7	Narrative devices
Wr11	Present information
Wr15	Express a view
Wr16	Validate an argument
Wr17	Informal advice
Wr19	Reflective writing

Year 8 objectives

Wd11	Figurative vocabulary
Wr6	Figurative language
Wr10	Effective information
Wr11	Explain complex ideas
Wr13	Present a case persuasively
Wr15	Advice about options
Wr16	Balanced analysis
Wr18	Critical review

Year 9 objectives

R12	Rhetorical devices
Wr6	Creativity in non-literary texts
Wr7	'Infotainment'
Wr9	Integrate information
Wr11	Descriptive detail
Wr14	Counter-argument
Wr15	Impartial guidance
Wr16	Balanced analysis

E. *Improving your narrative writing*

Aims of this unit of work

- To improve the quality of narration
- To improve the quality of characterisation and plotting in fiction
- To stimulate the imagination of the reader

Objectives addressed (by year)

Year 7 objectives

R6	Locate information
R8	Infer and deduce
R15	Endings
Wr5	Story structure
Wr6	Characterisation
Wr11	Present information
Wr14	Evocative description

Year 8 objectives

Wd11	Figurative vocabulary
R4	Versatile reading
R7	Implied and explicit meanings
R10	Development of key ideas
Wr5	Narrative commentary
Wr6	Figurative language
Wr11	Explain complex ideas

Year 9 objectives

R7	Compare texts
R11	Author's standpoint
Wr5	Narrative techniques
Wr6	Creativity in non-literary texts
Wr7	'Infotainment'
Wr11	Descriptive detail

All five units (A to E) are organised in four masterclasses of around 2 hours each for use by individuals or small groups working co-operatively.

1. Being more precise

In this masterclass you will learn how to:

- choose words for their exact meaning
- choose words for effect
- be specific.

Precision is the art of being exact and specific so that your reader knows exactly what you mean.

Choosing specific words

Some words have low value because they are so general and overused. Examples:

good/bad/okay	**go/went**	**say/said**
has/have/had	**get/got**	**do/does/did**

Activity 1: Wordwatch

Get into a group of no more than four. Take turns to talk about last weekend. The others should listen and 'buzz' whenever you say one of the words listed above. Ask them to suggest alternatives before starting again. Use this approach on yourself when you write.

One way of being more precise is choosing the word that gives most information.

- *Man* is more precise than *person*, but not as precise as *neighbour*.
- *Dog* is more precise than *animal*, but not as precise as *terrier*.
- *Infection* is more precise than *illness*, but not as precise as *influenza*.

Activity 2: Word-sharpening

Give more precise examples of:

Feeling	**Sealife**	**Food**	**Family**	**Games**	**Transport**

Go further and find even more precise examples for each new word.

Accurate description

When accuracy is important, people choose exact terms, as you do when you use scientific terminology in lessons. Accuracy is also important when you are trying to give a clear description of how something looks or works.

Here is a writer describing a piece of equipment that measures the height of the tide.

Activity 3: Describing a tide gauge

1 Read the extract.

Measuring the high tide

The old Admiralty gauge is in a wooden case with a clock-driven brass drum and a pen worked off a float. The float is mounted inside a pipe extending down into the water, called a stilling well because it is designed to damp down the motion of the waves. The sea has risen so high it has smashed the float right up against the top of the pipe and burst the seal. Callum experiences a jolt of alarm. The equipment in this hut is sited to catch any surge as it moves from the Atlantic into the North Sea. For it to explode the gauge like this means there must be a tide of unruly awesome dimensions forming out there.

From *Flood* by Richard Doyle

2 Draw and label the equipment using this description.

3 What helped you to understand what it looked like and how it worked?

4 Cover the extract but keep the sketch where you can see it. Use your own words to describe how the gauge measures the height of the tide.

Help ▶▶

Accurate description

- Use the right terminology.
- Explain what lies behind the terms.
- Elsewhere, keep to simple vocabulary.
- Explain things step by step.
- Choose verbs carefully to suggest why things are as they are.
- Use short direct sentences.
- Keep to the point.

Sounding sure

Being precise makes you sound confident and convincing.

Activity 4: Sounds convincing

1 Spot the convincing touches in this extract:

Closing the Thames Barrier to control a flood

It is time to close the Barrier. Such is the power of the hydraulics, it is possible to slam the gates shut in under five minutes but this would send a reflected wave downstream, causing severe flooding in the lower parts of the estuary. As a general rule, therefore, closure begins four hours before High Water.

There is also traffic on the river to be considered. With bad weather forecast and a closure due, shipping companies operating on the Thames are anxious to get their vessels up or downstream. Barrier Control is liaising with the Port of London Authority to let as many as possible through. Then there are the waste barges. A great part of the city's rubbish is loaded onto barges and taken to landfill sites down the estuary. This avoids having it trucked through London's streets. If the refuse companies can't use their barges, and rubbish is still coming in, they have to take a decision to divert it onto the roads. It is Barrier policy to be helpful in this matter.

From *Flood* by Richard Doyle

Help ▶▶

Convincing touches
Readers are reassured by:

- terminology, because it suggests the writer is knowledgeable

- detail, which make it sound well-researched

- facts and figures, because we believe hard information

- inside knowledge of processes as well as facts, because it suggests the writer is writing from personal experience

- a simple, direct style which suggests it's obvious and well-understood.

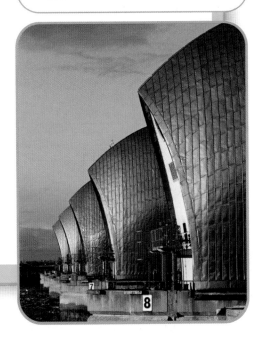

2 Identify three or four convincing touches that make the writer sound well-informed.

3 Write a convincing paragraph which explains how Dingbobs are created on a production line, and why they have become cheaper over the years. (It is up to you to invent the Dingbob.)

Choosing powerful verbs

An easy way to bring sharpness and focus to your writing is to choose precise and powerful verbs.

Activity 5: Understanding the power of verbs

1 Find the five verbs in these two sentences from a novel:

Storm by the sea

The storm is pounding the outer piers relentlessly. As each roller comes driving in, the sea heaves up and avalanches over, burying wall and pier.

From *Flood* by Richard Doyle

2 Give two reasons why each verb is effective in this context.

3 Suggest powerful verbs that might fit in these spaces:

Lifeboat in a storm

The boat is _____1_____ in the swell, burying her sides as she _____2_____ . Her searchlights _____3_____ out into the tossing crests. The bows _____4_____ up and _____5_____ steeply down into a trough. Another roller _____6_____ over the piers. The lights cut off abruptly. The lifeboat vanishes from sight, just disappears as if it has been _____7_____ out.

From *Flood* by Richard Doyle

Compare your answers with the writer's original choices at the end of this masterclass.

Help ▶▶

Powerful verbs

Verbs can be powerful because they:

- imply strength, aggression or force
- sound like the action
- contain sharp and plosive sounds such as *b* and *p*
- have harsh meanings
- are particular and precise
- have double meaning
- followed by prepositions such as *up*, *down* and *out*, which increase the sense of motion and direction.

Equally, verbs can be chosen to suggest calm, excitement, danger or any other emotion or mood.

Activity 6: Writing with powerful verbs

1   Write a paragraph describing the lifeboat making its way through the stormy sea. Choose your verbs to suggest the power of the storm.

2   Write another paragraph describing a sailing boat making its way through a still sea. Choose your verbs to suggest the calm.

Helping the verb

The verb gets a helping hand from the words around it and from its own sound effects.

Adverbs add to verbs. They usually end in *–ly*.

Prepositions are sometimes part of the verb, e.g. *to pass OUT, to sweep UP, to move ON*. Together the words are called a **verb phrase**.

Onomatopoeia is when verbs sound like the action described, e.g. *squelch, splatter, boom*.

Activity 7: Word search

Find the following words in the extracts about storms on the opposite page.

*   Find three adverbs, and explain how they add to the power of the verb.
*   Find five verb phrases in the two extracts, and explain how they add to the sense of movement.
*   Find two onomatopoeic verbs in the two extracts.

►► Test it))

Describe the launching of a lifeboat in a storm in about seven sentences.

What you get marks for

Use of powerful verbs (1 mark each)	up to 4 marks
Use of convincing details (1 mark each)	up to 4 marks
The overall effect is exciting and convincing	up to 2 marks
Total	**10 marks**

ANSWERS

Lifeboat in a storm

1 corkscrewing
2 rolls
3 stab
4 rear
5 plunge
6 cascades
7 blotted

2. Being more concise

In this masterclass you will learn how to:

- write concisely
- avoid over-generalising
- use brevity to your advantage.

Introduction

Concise writing is short but to the point. Concision is important when:

- there is little time
- there is little space
- your audience won't wait
- detail and description are unnecessary.

When you have few words, you have to decide how to keep it short:

- by covering everything by being general
- by using a typical example instead of covering everything
- by going straight to the heart of the matter, the main issue.

Here's the opening of a book about saving the environment by shopping wisely.

> Every day of the week, whether we are shopping for simple necessities or for luxury items, for fish fingers or for fur coats, we are making choices that affect the environmental quality of the world we live in.

From _The Green Consumer Guide_ by John Elkington and Julia Hailes

This is a good example of concision because it makes a point of principle in a small space, and adds in some specific details that make it real and everyday.

Activity 1: Effective explanation

1   What is effective about the language in this explanation?

> Few of us can spot the links between what we do day-to-day and the environmental destruction which is happening around the world. Most fast-fooders know little – and care less – about the loss of the world's tropical forests. Yet almost two-fifths of the deforestation of Brazil from the mid 1970s to the mid 1990s was caused by the clearance of forests for cattle ranching. Much of the beef produced was destined for fast food hamburgers.

From *The Green Consumer Guide* by John Elkington and Julia Hailes

2   In one sentence of your own, explain the link between hamburgers and the death of the rainforest.

Concise explanations

If you only have one sentence, it helps to:

Start with the **effect**.

Follow it with the **cause**, using a connective such as *because, on account of* or *is the result of.*

Follow it with a **link** between cause and effect, using a connective such as *which in turn, causing* or *resulting in.*

If you need to make another link, use another sentence.

Example

Rain falls from the clouds *because* the wind blown in from the sea carries millions of tiny water droplets into the cold high air of the hills, *causing* the droplets to gather into raindrops too heavy to hang in the air.

Activity 2: Making a difference

1 In 50 to 60 words, persuade reluctant readers that they can make a difference by choosing to buy goods that are environment-friendly.

2 When you have done this, read the original 55 words from the book on page 12. Consider how you and the writer have tried to be concise.

Choosing smart examples

One of the tricks of concise writing is not to give every detail but to give the typical and most telling examples.If they are *typical*, you can use one example to represent many more. *Revealing* examples show why something is significant and challenge the reader to see things in a new light.

Activity 3: Examples

Here is a chart showing the amount of waste we throw away each year.

If you were trying to make a concise point about our wasteful lifestyle, which examples would you use, and why?

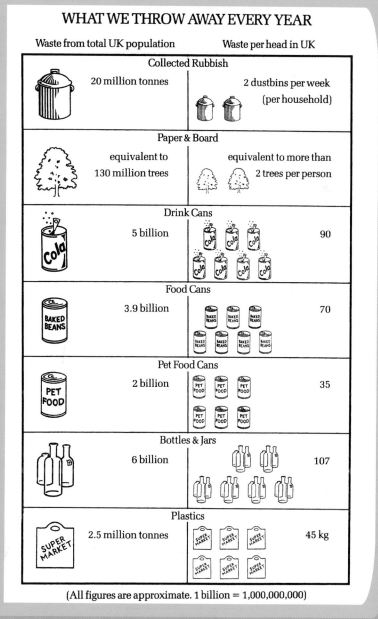

WHAT WE THROW AWAY EVERY YEAR

Waste from total UK population — Waste per head in UK

| Collected Rubbish | |
| 20 million tonnes | 2 dustbins per week (per household) |

| Paper & Board | |
| equivalent to 130 million trees | equivalent to more than 2 trees per person |

| Drink Cans | |
| 5 billion | 90 |

| Food Cans | |
| 3.9 billion | 70 |

| Pet Food Cans | |
| 2 billion | 35 |

| Bottles & Jars | |
| 6 billion | 107 |

| Plastics | |
| 2.5 million tonnes | 45 kg |

(All figures are approximate. 1 billion = 1,000,000,000)

From *The Green Consumer Guide* by John Elkington and Julia Hailes

Making a point

Activity 4: Junk mail

- Spend two minutes listing all the types of junk mail that arrive in your home.

- Spend two minutes listing all the reasons that make junk mail a bad thing that should be banned.

- Spend two minutes considering why it might be hard to ban junk mail.

Make a concise argument about the evils of junk mail that will persuade readers to remove their names from national mailing lists. Your words have to fit in a 9cm by 6cm box (like the one below), to appear in a local newspaper.

NO MORE JUNK MAIL

**Remove your name from mailing lists by
XXXXX**

Activity 5: Leftovers

- Observe what happens to leftovers from school dinners and lunchboxes each lunchtime in your school.
- Come up with a list of suggestions for reducing the waste.
- Choose the best ones to include in a proposal explaining the problem and outlining your solutions to the school council or headteacher.
- Write the proposal in no more 100 words.

Activity 6: *Not in my backyard*

You are watching a debate on television about a protest over building a waste incinerator in a town 75km away. Protestors against the incinerator are claiming that it would be much better placed in *your* area, because no one will mind having it there. The presenter invites viewers to send in their opinions by email, which can be flashed on the screen during the programme.

- Write an email of less than 25 words which brings out the principle as well as answering the point.

>> Test it)))

Use the information below to help you to write approximately 75 words explaining to people why and how they need to save water.

WATER IN THE HOME

Problems with fresh water
Keeping it clean
Clearing up pollution
Drought in the dry season
Cost of treating waste
Preventing flooding
Leaking and burst pipes

How much water it takes to:

Flush a toilet	10 litres
Take a bath	80 litres
Take a shower	30 litres
Use a washing machine	100 litres
Use a dishwasher	50 litres
Water a typical lawn	10 litres per minute

Each person uses around 50,000 litres of water a year.

What you get marks for

For keeping to 70–80 words	2 marks
For explaining persuasively the need to save water	2 marks
For using 2 or 3 telling examples	2 marks
For giving 2 or 3 clear instructions for saving water	2 marks
For an overall effect that is pithy, persuasive and strong	2 marks
Total	**10 marks**

ANSWERS

Making a difference (in 55 words)

Don't just grin and bear it. As consumers, we have real power to effect change. We can ask questions about supply and manufacture. We can request new or different products. And we can use our ultimate power, voting with our feet and wallets – either buying a product somewhere else or not buying it at all.

From *The Green Consumer Guide* by John Elkington and Julia Hailes

3. Making your point

In this masterclass you will learn how to:

- justify a point
- draw out a conclusion
- drive your point home.

Making a point

Here is a plan for making a point:

1 Introduce it.

2 Explain it.

3 Justify it.

4 Draw out the conclusion.

5 Drive it home.

You may not need all five steps, or you may use a step more than once.

Example:

1. Introduces the point

2. Explains the point

3. Justifies the point

Shops could do more to help the environment by wrapping only in paper. Instead of plastic bags, goods should be wrapped in cheap recycled paper or held in thick paper carrier bags. We know this would work because that is how it did work before plastic bags were introduced less than fifty years ago. Paper decomposes safely in the waste, or it can be recycled, saving the cost and pollution that is created by plastic bags that cannot be destroyed. Plastic is, unfortunately, for ever.

5. Drives it home

4. Draws out the point

Justifying a point

Justifying a point means showing that it is fair and true by:

- giving reasons why it is the best thing to do
- reminding people how they would behave in the same situation
- providing evidence that it is true
- making a moral argument
- showing that the alternatives are worse.

Evidence might include:

- statistics
- facts
- the word of a witness
- an expert opinion
- a quotation
- close logic explained
- an example
- a case study.

Activity 1: Justifying a point

Which two techniques does this paragraph use to justify its point?

Advice to managers

If there's a trainee in your workplace, try to give her interesting tasks to do as well as the jobs you'd rather eat bees than do yourself. Remember, she's there for some experience in your field, not just to do clerical work. Most will be very happy if their jobs are a combination of drudgery and interesting work they can boast about later. If you have benefited from the helpfulness of a trainee, don't forget it. She did not type up your contact list just for the sheer thrill of it. Be willing to write letters of reference or allow your name to be added to her CV.

From *The Fabulous Girl's Guide to Decorum* by Kim Izo and Ceri Marsh

Check your answers at the end of the masterclass.

Activity 2: Make a point

Write these paragraphs using at least three steps in the plan for making a point.

1 A paragraph that says why all secondary pupils have to read at least one Shakespeare play.

2 A paragraph that persuades pupils that it is not wrong to 'shop' bullies.

3 A paragraph that persuades people to buy a particular chocolate bar.

Drawing out a conclusion

It is helpful to round up with a short clear summary of the point you are making. This is the easiest way to make sure that what is obvious to you is also obvious to the reader. It is the moment when you 'get to the point'.

Look at the last line in this paragraph:

Italians and children

Visitors to Italy, bewitched by the ease with which small children are accommodated and tolerated in restaurants, tend to believe that the Italians love children. Surely this is the best country in the world to have a child, or to be one?

Amanda Craig in the *Observer*, 25 May 2003

Notice how it makes the point directly (*this is the best country in the world to have a child*) and adds force to the message by making it a question so the reader is invited to agree.

Activity 3: Adding conclusions

1 Here is a paragraph from which the last line has been omitted. Suggest a good conclusion.

The planet Mars

Take a careful look at the night sky this summer and watch out for a distinctive bright red dot near the constellation Aquarius, to the south. If you can, get hold of a telescope and study this little world. Note its distinctive dark markings and strange ochre-coloured patches. Mark its white-capped poles. You will never get a chance for such detailed scrutiny again, for on 28 August, Mars – the ancient Babylonian Star of Death, the Roman Bringer of War – will swing closer to Earth than at any other time in recorded history. XXXXXXXXXXXXXXXXXXXXXXXXXXXXXXXXXX.

Robin McKie in the *Observer*, 25 May 2003

2 Compare your sentence with others in your class. What different techniques do they use to conclude?

3 Look at the end of this masterclass for the original wording used by the writer. What technique does he use?

Driving home your point

1. Sound confident

Introduce your points with confident phrases. For example:

Certainly,...   The fact is that...

There is no doubt that,...   Clearly,...

2. Put poetry into your language

For example alliteration is used here to end a paragraph about shopping:

Suddenly, greed is good.

From *The Fabulous Girl's Guide to Decorum* by Kim Izo and Ceri Marsh

Help ▶▶

Drawing out a conclusion

• Summarise your main points.

• Keep it pithy.

• Use commonplace words.

• Make it sound like common sense.

• Sound confident.

• Use opening sentences that set up the point you are going to make at the end.

• Draft the closing sentence before you write the paragraph, so that you work up to it.

3. Generalise

Sum up so that you lead the reader from particular detail to general truths.

Modern funerals

The week before, Roslyn tells me, she oversaw a woodland funeral attended by two busloads of friends and family. They sang African songs instead of saying prayers, buried the body themselves, then partied around the grave long into the night on champagne and wine. 'It seemed,' she adds, 'so much healthier.'

Sean O'Hagan in the *Observer*, 18 May 2003

4. End on a question

Don't overuse this one. A question is a clever way to make the reader think.

The Beagle

On Monday 2 June, the UK's *Beagle 2* – a £30m probe the size of a bicycle wheel – will be blasted into space and propelled towards the heavens strapped to its mothercraft. In seven months, the pair will begin a series of experiments aimed at answering one simple question: are we alone?

Robin McKie in the *Observer*, 25 May 2003

5. Put a sting in the tail

Sting-in-the-tail endings are short, curt and have shock value. They work like the punchline of a joke. Here, for example, is the ending of a newspaper article about the life of MPs:

Politicians endure long hours, job insecurity and daily abuse for the privilege of promoting the public good and a better world. Or so they say.

Politicians endure long hours, job insecurity and daily abuse for the privilege of promoting the public good and a better world. Or so they say.

Test it

Write these two paragraphs to bring out clearly their key points:

1   You answer complaints about trains. Write a paragraph explaining politely to an angry passenger why all your trains are 'no smoking'.

2   Write a one-paragraph letter to a Sunday newspaper (which come in several parts) objecting to its new 'shrink-wrap' plastic packaging because of the threat to the environment.

What you get marks for

Paragraph 1 (trains)

The point is explained	1 mark
The point is justified	1 mark
The point of principle is drawn out	1 mark
It is clear and simple, sounds like common sense	1 mark
It uses confident words, sounds sure	1 mark

Paragraph 2 (plastic wrapping)

The point is explained	1 mark
The point is justified	1 mark
The point of principle is drawn out	1 mark
The conclusion packs a punch	2 marks
Total	**10 marks**

ANSWERS

Justifying a point

1   Moral argument (a reminder of her aims in taking the job) – *she's there for some experience in your field.*

2   Reminder of how you would behave in same situation (because this gives you an insight into her feelings) – *She did not type up your contact list just for the sheer thrill of it.*

Final line of The planet Mars paragraph

The last time Mars got this near, men were still hunting mammoths.

4. Editing down

In this masterclass you will learn how to:

- shorten your writing
- summarise your writing
- abbreviate your writing.

Introduction

There are three ways to shorten writing:

- by cutting things out
- by saying it in fewer words
- by abbreviating.

Activity 1: Methods for shortening

The following sentence was shortened by cutting out the examples and by compressing two phrases into one.

A variety of illnesses such a malaria and even bubonic plague are carried by insects and transmitted when they bite.

A variety of illnesses are transmitted by insects.

- Find the examples that were deleted.
- Explain how the two phrases were compressed into one.

What methods are used to shorten the next sentence?

The introduction to your essay is very good – lively, some interesting turns of phrase and clear explanations.

Intro is v. good – lively and well-expressed.

Cutting things out

Cutting things out is easily done, especially at a computer. It's choosing what to cut that is hard. It all depends on:

- how short you want it to be
- what is important to the meaning.

Activity 2: Cutting out

Cut each of these sentences to about half their length:

1   Milly, my younger sister, can't sit still for more than a minute before she starts wriggling and fidgeting.

2   The best shopping is for games, especially computer software, and the worst shopping is for clothes because that takes hours.

3   The body of an insect is divided into three main sections: the head, the thorax (which is the chest) and the abdomen (which is the lower body).

- Discuss how you decided what to cut out.
- How did you choose between *Milly* and *my younger sister*? *Thorax* and *chest*?
- Would you have made different choices in sentence 1 if you had been writing the first line of a children's bedtime story?
- Would you have made different choices in sentence 3 if the main point of the writing was to explain the specialist words?
- Give examples of where it is possible to cut out the odd word because the sentence can manage without them.

Help ▶▶

Common cuts

Here are some of the things that commonly get cut:

- repetitions
- information that appears elsewhere in slightly different form, e.g. names and roles
- examples
- details
- obvious things that the reader will already know
- asides such as personal comments
- less important information
- 'speech'.

Writers often have to cut down their writing to fit in the space available. This book has been written to fit into double-page spreads. Newspaper journalists write to fit a story into available columns. You have to do it when you fill in answer boxes in tests.

Activity 3: Newspaper edit

Here is a newspaper story. There is not enough space in the newspaper for all of it. Cut it down to half its length.

Magician's London debut in glass coffin

He has been encased in ice and he has withstood 35 hours on top of a 80ft pole, but for his next trick, David Blaine says that he will endure 44 days without food in a glass coffin by the Thames.

The New York illusionist, 30, will crawl into a clear plexi-glass box, measuring 7ft long by 7ft tall by 3ft wide and endure starvation in solitary confinement. While Blaine promises to suffer in silence, he is likely to become London's most unusual tourist attraction for the six weeks that he is suspended by crane near Tower Bridge.

'It will be a public isolation that I will have to endure by adapting and surviving as an animal would: on instinct,' he said. 'There will be no trickery and no means of escape'

Blaine will have one set of clothes and a blanket. He said he would take no food and will receive only water through a feeding tube. He will communicate with no one and his bodily functions will be catered for by a small backpack containing nappies and a tube to urinate in.

His first plan for a London debut was to emulate his hero, the escapologist Harry Houdini, by being chained up and thrown in the Thames, but the London authorities were nervous about this plan.

Adam Smith in *The Times*, 20 August 2003

Help >>

Editing

Read the article first so you know what it's about and what is important to the meaning. Don't try to do it 'as you go'.

There are some rules when you write in a newspaper:
- Give both sides.
- Keep a fair balance.
- Give an overview first.
- Make the facts interesting.

Saying it in fewer words

The alternative to cutting things out, is to say them in fewer words by generalising, condensing or compressing.

Generalising means giving an overview. You lose the detail but you hold on to the main idea. For example:

> **Out of 20 people surveyed, 18 enjoyed watching television. One did not like watching television, and one was uncertain.**
>
> **The survey showed that almost everyone enjoys television.**

Condensing means using a smarter word to avoid long explanations. For example:

> **He always had a quick temper and was often snappy with people.**
>
> **He was irritable.**

Compressing means squeezing out unnecessary words. You rewrite in a plainer style. For example:

> **The hole-in-the-wall cash till offers the customer a quick and easy way to carry out everyday transactions without ever stepping into a bank.**
>
> **Hole-in-the-wall cash tills are quick and easy to use without visiting the bank.**

Activity 4: Using fewer words

Reduce each of these sentences to half their length:

1 My mother has six brothers, two sisters and twenty nieces and nephews.
2 With no first-aid equipment, they used a thin belt to bind his broken arm to a thick wooden stick and then they knotted a spare shirt around his neck so that, when he stood up, his arm would be supported in the loop.

Afterwards, find sample answers at the end of this masterclass.

Abbreviating

Abbreviating means shortening by using note form. The trick is to leave just enough to remember what you meant. You can:

- leave out 'grammatical' words
- cut out unnecessary words
- shorten words
- list
- use bullet points
- use diagrams if it helps.

Another example:

> John, would you mind bringing Emma home from the cinema at 8.00pm? Thanks, Sarah.
>
> J.
>
> Plse collect Em from cinema at 8.
>
> S.

People tend to move house for three main reasons: first, the family needs different accommodation when they marry, have children, divorce or lose a family member; second, their financial circumstances change when they get a job, lose a job or retire; and third, they sometimes need to move to be nearer to a job, a relative or a place they love.

Main reasons for moving:
- **family change (marry, divorce, die)**
- **financial change (get and lose jobs, retire)**
- **to be somewhere else (job, love).**

Activity 5: Abbreviation

Shorten this advice to half its length by putting it into note form:

Keeping dogs in their place

It's a mistake to allow your dog to sleep on the bed or even in the bedroom. It encourages him to think that he is your equal, and if he thinks this then soon he will forget that you're in charge and he will start competing. Make your dog sleep in his own bed. For the same reason, don't allow him up on the sofa because it will raise his status. Don't give him food as you eat and never give him the last piece of food. Don't let him win every game. He will think that he's the boss and treat you as the underdog.

▶ Test it))))

Reduce the following article to about half its length. Try to retain the main ideas. Use full sentences and do not abbreviate.

Never forget that a dog is a descendant of the wolf. He still has a wild streak. In the wild, dogs live in packs and they fight for their place in the pack. Top dogs get the first food and lead the pack. Lower dogs have to wait for food and follow the others.

Well-trained dogs look to their owners as top dogs. Trouble starts when a dog thinks he is top dog. Without meaning to, you can give your dog big ideas. For example, if you pamper him, let him eat your food, win games or come into your bedroom, he will think you are weak and that he can challenge you. Small children are most at risk because the dog may feel stronger than them.

You can soon spot a dog that thinks he is the master. He will start to bite, refuse commands, try to take food and jump up on furniture.

What you get marks for

The article is now half its original length	4 marks
The link to wild behaviour is still there	2 marks
The main idea of thinking himself top dog is still there	2 marks
The overall effect is sensible and fluent	2 marks
Total	**10 marks**

ANSWERS

Saying it in fewer words

1   My mother comes from a large family.

2   They improvised a splint using a belt and a stick, and an arm bandage using a spare shirt.

5. Marshalling your ideas

In this masterclass you will learn how to:

- organise your ideas ready for writing
- sequence your ideas
- consider different ways of presenting ideas.

Most language follows an order. For example, stories and instructions are based on chronological order; debates and interviews are based on alternating from one view to another; reports often start with the most important facts and then work down to less important facts. But some forms of writing, such as information, analysis and discussion, have no fixed order. You have to plan ahead how to shape the writing.

Organising ideas ready for writing

There are five simple things you can do to organise ideas for writing

1

Scope it

Think about what to cover

2

Gather ideas

Generate ideas – big or small, one-off or linked, general ideas or specific details

3

Cluster ideas

Link together similar or linked ideas

4

Select ideas

Remove weak ideas

5

Sequence ideas

Put the ideas in the best order for writing

Activity 1: Lunchtime Survival Guide

Prepare to write a *Lunchtime Survival Guide* for new pupils starting at school.

1 Scope it

- Ask yourself: who will read this and what will they want to know?
- Information about school dinners is bound to be useful, but would you want to tell them about the outbreak of food poisoning last year?
- You'll want to suggest some ways to pass the time, but will you tell them about lunchtime activities that break the school rules?
- Write down a list of three to five things you should cover.

2 Gather ideas

- Use a pencil so you can rearrange ideas if you see a pattern emerging.
- Jot ideas around a clean sheet. Write important ideas close to the centre, but less important ideas further away. Write similar ideas close to each other.
- Cross out ideas that are repeated or don't work.

3 Cluster ideas

- Draw lines or arrows to link ideas.
- Put big circles around clusters (or colour them with the same highlighter).
- Give titles to the big clusters and write them in.

4 Select ideas

- Select the important ideas.
- Delete less important ideas.

5 Sequence ideas

- Put the big clusters in a good order for writing. Put the main ones first.

1. <u>Lunch</u> (because that's the main reason for having lunchtime and the first thing people want to do)

2. <u>**Things to do outside and what happens if it rains**</u> (could swap with 3)

3. <u>**Things to do inside – library and clubs**</u> (could swap with 2)

4. <u>**Help if things go wrong**</u> (don't put bad things first because they would worry a newcomer)

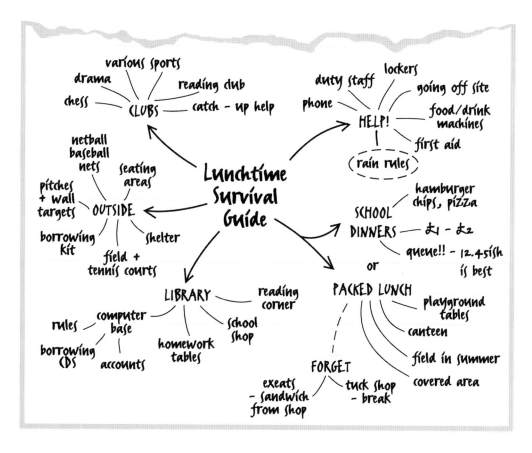

Activity 2: Organising an event

Scope, gather, cluster, select and sequence ideas for a magazine article about organising an event or visit such as:

- organising a birthday party for small children
- arranging to watch an away game
- organising a camping trip.

Different ways of presenting ideas

The *Lunchtime Survival Guide* could have been tackled in these ways:

1 **As questions and answers: How do I get a school dinner? What sort of things do they serve? etc.**

2 **As case studies: Paul, who likes to get a quick lunch then get homework done; Shiani, who likes to get out and be with her friends, etc.**

Help ▶▶

Different ways of organising work

- step by step
- timetable
- case studies, e.g. Day in the life of...
- debate for and against
- going through key issues
- comparing or contrasting
- in order of importance
- A–Z.

Help ▶▶

Hit lists

Possible titles for hit lists:

- Ten good reasons to...
- Ten amazing facts about...
- Ten top tips for...
- Ten ways to...
- Ten simple steps for better...

Help ▶▶

Different forms of writing

- letter
- magazine article
- newspaper report
- information leaflet
- brochure, guide or manual
- timetable or timeline
- diary, journal or log
- factfile or grid.

Activity 3: Arranging ideas

Suggest different ways of arranging:

- information about Henry VIII
- information about dragonflies
- your plan for organising the event or visit.

Deciding on the structure

If there is no obvious order for your points, you need to decide on a way to structure your writing.

Activity 4: Structuring leaflets

A pet shop offers a set of leaflets to customers:

- *Choosing a pet*, which compares the advantages and disadvantages of dogs, cats, hamsters, rabbits, fish and snakes as pets

- *Things to consider before buying your pet*, which advises customers about such things as cost, food, home, cleaning, safety, breeding and health

- *All about hamsters*, which gives customers plenty of detail about the history, habits, diseases and types of hamster available.

Discuss each title and think how you would structure each leaflet. Is there any particular order? How would you decide the sequence?

Help ▶▶

Structuring information

- Bear in mind the reader and what they need to know.
- Put the big, obvious, positive points first.
- Put problems last.
- Cluster smaller points together, if you can.
- History and background usually come early.
- Everyday things come before unusual things.
- Work hard on the links between points, so that it does not read like a list.

Activity 5: Links

Linking paragraphs on similar topics such as *dogs*, *cats*, *hamsters*, *rabbits*, *fish* and *snakes* is worth some care. Compare these links:

- My next topic is dogs.
- Next, fish.
- If dogs and cats sound too noisy and troublesome, then you might be happier with the calm and silent world of fish.
- The fifth choice is fish.
- So far, we've looked at animals you can take out and about and play with in your home. Now let's look at a pet that requires less energy.
- That's rabbits. Now on to fish.
- A more unusual pet for the adventurous pet owner is the snake.

Which ones work best and why?

Help ▶▶

Good links

- Refer back to the last topic.
- Look forward to the next topic.
- Stimulate some interest.
- Sound keen and enthusiastic.

>> Test it))

Plan and write a guide for pupils in Year 9 choosing which DT subject to study for GCSE, no longer than one side of A4 paper.

What you get marks for

A good plan which covers several subjects and considerations	2 marks
Organised around sensible topics	2 marks
Mentions things that people want to know when they choose a subject	2 marks
Has effective links between topics	2 marks
Overall effect	2 marks
Total	**10 marks**

6. *Composing in your head*

In this masterclass you will learn how to:

- map a piece of writing in your head
- hear the voice of the writing in your head
- compose the writing in your head as you go.

For many people, the hardest part of writing is the beginning. Others find that they run out of steam halfway through. Both of these problems can be solved if you learn how to plan 'in the head'. Planning in the head is quicker than waiting for inspiration that may never arrive.

Activity 1: Watching yourself write

Try this. You will be asked in a moment to write for five minutes, and notice as you write what you do inside and outside of your head. For example, you may pause, lose track or hear a voice 'dictating'.

1   The task: You have just been thrown into a prison cell. Write down your first impressions as you take in your new surroundings. Write for 5 minutes.

2   Think back, then jot down what processes you went through in your head as you wrote.

3   Turn over and compare your list with that in the box.

Help ▶▶

Composing in the head

Most people do these things:

- picture the things they write about, sometimes drawing on their own memories
- imagine how they would feel and react in the same situation
- remember experiences they have had
- recall what they know, e.g. about prisons
- hear their own voice composing parts of sentences
- hear the 'tone' or 'music' of the writing even if they do not have the exact words
- pick out something that strikes them to focus on
- sense the length and shape of what they will write
- find some words to start their sentences
- stop and think
- reread what they have written so far, to see what the effect is and how other readers might take it
- pause to organise the words before they write them down
- do 'business' – pencil sharpening, paper wiping, pen shaking
- lose their thread and go back to read themselves into the sentence again
- rehearse sentences or phrases before they write them down.

Activity 2: Factual writing

Repeat the first activity, but this time with factual writing. Your 5-minute task is to write a one-paragraph introduction to the library for pupils new to the school.

- Did you use the same strategies?
- Discuss what is different about writing non-fiction.
- Afterwards, look at answers at the end of this masterclass.

Mapping a piece of writing in the head

It is always a good idea to have in your head a map of the whole piece of writing. To do this, imagine the writing as a labelled shape. The shape should show the structure and topics. For example:

The race

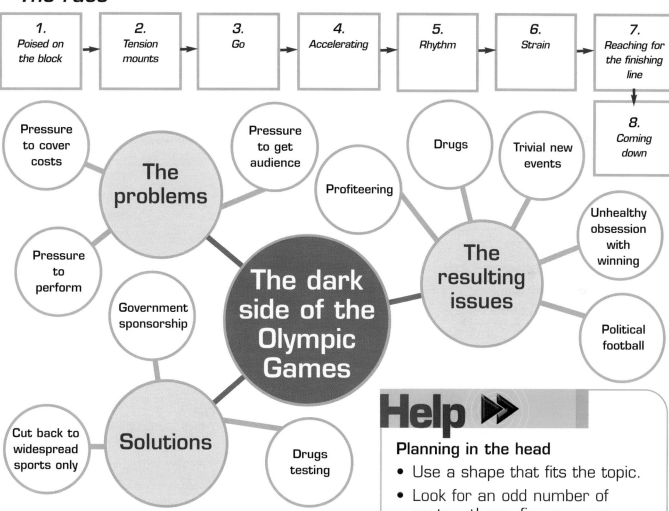

Activity 3: Writing map

1 Take two minutes to draw a map for a piece of writing on preventing bullying.

2 Compare your work with others and discuss which maps look easiest and best.

3 In your head, make a mental map for a piece of writing on 'Why is PE worth learning?' Do not write it down.

4 Discuss how you went about making the mental map.

Help ▶▶

Planning in the head

• Use a shape that fits the topic.

• Look for an odd number of parts – three, five or seven – so you can use the first and last boxes as introduction and conclusion.

• Each part might be a paragraph.

• Pay special attention to the links between points. Put effort into the links between paragraphs.

Finding a voice for your writing

The content of your writing is less important than the way you tell it.
This means choosing the right style, tone and type of language.
Here is a way to hit on the right voice:

1   Remember examples you have met before.
2   Copy the style by composing the opening sentence in your head.
3   If you don't know the right style, think about it logically: who are you writing for and why? Fit the style to suit the reader and the purpose.

Working out the right voice

Things to think about:

- level of formality
- personal or impersonal approach
- first or third person
- level of detail
- specialised or general vocabulary
- tone of voice
- simple sentences or elaborate expressions
- active sentences or passive sentences.

Activity 4: Make your own writing frame

Write down some typical

- opening lines
- closing lines
- links between sections

that might be used for

- a news bulletin
- a children's bedtime story
- a letter of complaint
- a resort described in a holiday brochure.

Composing in the head

Good writers have four things in their head at any moment in writing:

- a map of the content and structure of the writing
- a feel for the style and voice they are going to use
- the opening words of the sentence they are on
- a clear idea of the length of the sentence and how it ends.

When they are faced with a writing task, the first thing they do is to think about what they know about the topic and what they will cover. But they move very quickly to consider how they will shape this information into chunks for the reader. Very quickly, they see the four or five main things they want to say, the rough order in which they will say them, and the overall 'shape' of the writing. In other words, they have a good idea how the writing will go.

As they write, they stop now and then to read back what they have written to check that they are on the right lines. They are also listening to the 'voice' to hear if it sounds right. They listen for false notes and then they correct them.

Good writers have an impression of how each sentence will sound and how it will end, even if the detail is not yet worded. They are guided by a mental outline of the sentence, and by the rhythm and voice; they keep 'in tune'. When they look for words, they look for ones that will fit and sound right.

Good writers draft in their heads. They fish around for words that will fit but sometimes they can hear that they don't, so they discard these words and try again, or play with the words to see if they can be made to fit. They test alternatives until they hit on some that work.

Activity 5: A quick plan

1 You have exactly 3 minutes to **plan** this task. Write nothing. Compose in your head the outline of a paragraph of four or five sentences which explains why it is that the vast majority of pupils, when asked how they would vote in a general election, say they would vote for the same party as their parents.

2 Now you have exactly 2 minutes to **write** your plan.

3 Discuss how it turned out. What did you find hard? What worked? If you had been allowed to write three or four words down to help you plan, would it have helped?

The teacher will time you on this test.

1 You have 5 minutes for this. Draw a planning map for an article about dangerous sports for a colour supplement magazine.

2 You have 2 minutes to plan in your head a paragraph which argues either for or against banning boxing as a dangerous sport. Do not write it until you are told to.

3 You have 1 minute to jot down the paragraph plan.

4 You now have 3 minutes to write the paragraph.

What you get marks for

For the plan

For completing the plan	1 mark
For planning three good, sound points	2 marks
For including some ideas to put into each section	2 marks

For the paragraph

The paragraph is complete	1 mark
The paragraph keeps up the voice it is written in	1 mark
The paragraph makes two or three good points well	2 marks
The paragraph feels 'whole'	1 mark
Total	**10 marks**

ANSWERS

For factual writing you have to:

* place greater emphasis on what you know than what you feel
* think how to organise the information because it doesn't unfold in order of event like a story
* pay more attention to the needs of the readers and think about how you relate to them
* stick with a particular way of writing that you know will fit in a school booklet.

7. Processing your material

In this masterclass you will learn how to:

- select what you need from different sources
- integrate them into a single piece of writing
- find a style that works for them all.

When you combine information from different sources, you can end up with a crazy mix of prose, notes, lists, tables, formal writing and personal writing. The challenge is to integrate them into a coherent piece of writing.

The process

Follow this process to make the work as easy as possible:

Step 1 ➡ Imagine in advance the length and structure of the finished piece.

Step 2 ➡ List the headings you will use, leaving 10cm between each heading.

Step 3 ➡ Consider what information you will need under each heading and where you think you may find it.

Step 4 ➡ Find the information, highlighting the details you need, and assemble keyword notes under each heading.

Step 5 ➡ Take each group of notes, and merge the points together into a single plan.

Step 6 ➡ Write a full draft quickly in one style.

Activity 1: A day out in Guildford

Create a leaflet suggesting ideas for a day out in Guildford for one adult and three children aged between 7 and 9 using the steps shown on page 37. Steps 1 and 2 have been done for you.

Steps to take	Example: A day out in Guildford	
Step 1 Decide in advance a rough idea of the finished piece	An A5 leaflet made from an A4 folded sheet which suggests activities for kids, gives useful information, and is written in a relaxed, user-friendly style.	
Step 2 List the headings you will use, leaving 10cm between each	1 About Guildford 3 Map 5 Things to do 7 Things to do if it rains	2 How to get there 4 What to see 6 Where to eat

Now follow Steps 3 to 6, using the Help boxes if you get stuck. Use the information on pages 39 and 40 or look it up on the internet, in the library, or tourist office to find information.

Making notes

- Only write down as much as you need.

- Keep your notes to short key words – this will help you to express them in your own way later.

- Reorder and re-express points so they are ready to use.

Highlighting information

- Mark pages with Post-it notes.

- Write in light pencil so you can change it or rub it out later.

- Have in your head a list of things to look for, e.g. place, time, cost.

- Scan quickly by using sub-headings.

- Don't waste time reading every word – skim through it.

- Look out for key words.

- If you are keeping notes on two or three things, avoid confusion by using different colours or marking systems, e.g. underlining, circling.

<u>Walks</u>

- River Wey – Alice in Wonderland written on bank near cinema (scene with rabbit) – Lewis Carroll public right of way – bronze statue – guided tours Thursdays at 2 if fine – statue, picnic seat

- Wetland walk – start Burpham A3 exit – canal towpath, lake, boardwalk through marsh – wildlife reserve – ends at canal lock

- Ghost walk – evening 7pm – meet at The Angel – £5 each/£2 children – 2 miles – guided tour with local stories

- Newlands Corner – spectacular views, café

- Town centre trail – Guildhall, undercroft, medieval castle, almshouses, Dapdune Wharf – free leaflet tourist office in Tunsgate

GUILDFORD MUSEUM
Castle Arch, Guildford GUI 3SX
Tel: 01483 444750
www.guildfordmuseum.org
Step into the world of Prehistoric man, the Romans and Saxons, monks and friars, Lewis Carroll and the Victorians when you visit Guildford Museum. The archaeology gallery shows the development of life in Surrey from Prehistoric times to the Middle Ages.

GUILDFORD BOAT HOUSE
Millbrook, Guildford GUI 3JX
Tel: 01483 504494
email: info@guildfordboats.co.uk
www.guildfordboats.co.uk
Take to the water on the beautiful River Wey: Rowing boats for hire and river trips from the centre of Guildford. Traditionally shaped narrow boats are also available to charter for short breaks or longer.

History of Guildford

An essential resting place for travellers for hundreds of years, the historic town of Guildford is still a vital part of any itinerary for visitors to the South East.

Guildford's traditional High Street helps to maintain the unique ambience of the town. An excellent range of shops can be found behind the traditional frontages of historic buildings. On Fridays and Saturdays a traditional street market operates in the town's North Street. Once a month the High Street is filled with the stalls of the Farmers' Market and for two weeks in July a Craft Market is held during the Guildford Summer Festival.

Guided walks of the town explore the history of the area, visiting the Guildhall with its famous projecting clock and Abbot's Hospital. A short walk from the High Street is the castle built by William the Conqueror. All that remains of Surrey's only Royal Castle is its ruined keep, set in a spectacular garden. Nearby is The Chestnuts, where Lewis Carroll often stayed. The Chestnuts is privately owned but you may visit his grave in the Mount Cemetery and two statues (in the Castle grounds and by the River Wey) celebrate his work and links with the town. Returning to the High Street the walking tour visits a medieval undercroft, this was originally a shop beneath a shop and now houses an exhibition. The River Wey is at the bottom of the High Street and the Yvonne Arnaud Theatre has a lovely riverside setting.

Synthesising different styles

The biggest challenge lies in pulling together the different voices and different formats into one style. Avoid a 'cut and paste' approach. It is easier to start with a new idea and slot the information into it. This way, your work is more likely to sound coherent and 'yours'.

Activity 2: Guildford Castle

Here is information about Guildford Castle from three different sources. Fold an A3 sheet of paper into tall sections to create a three-part leaflet. Use just one side of it to tell primary school visitors about the castle.

Source 1: A photograph of Guildford castle

Source 2: A textbook

Guildford Castle was built alongside the Saxon town on a ridge commanding both the river crossing and the possible approach to the Thames Valley through the river gap. It was the only castle in royal hands in either Sussex or Surrey, which was why it became the residence of the sheriff, the chief agent for royal administration. As with many castles, when more resources became available, greater use was made of stone for building, which improved security, and attention was also given to providing comfort.

In the wider history of England, Guildford Castle's only notable military event was its capture by the French heir to the throne, Dauphin Louis, in June 1216.

Later, Warwick Castle at Kingston was built. Known only from documents and maps, it may have been erected to defend the river crossing shortly before it was captured by Henry III in 1264.

At Lingfield, Starborough Castle had substantial fortifications along with a water-filled moat. Licence to crenellate was granted to Sir Reginald Cobham in 1341 and a drawing by Hollar shows a building not unlike Bodiam Castle in East Sussex, with four towers and a gatehouse.

From *Hidden Depths* by Roger Hunt

Source 3: A guide to Guildford for disabled visitors

The castle grounds

On the wall of the Tunsgate shopping precinct is the Edward and Eleanor sundial, erected in 1972 to commemorate Guildford's 13th century connections with the Crown. Take the path around the left-hand side of the bowling green, where you will find seats. At the end, the path turns right and continues down a slope into the ornamental gardens at the foot of...

The castle keep

This was build in the 12th century but the remains of earlier Norman walls can be seen on the slope of the mound; they are built of chalk which was quarried locally, while the keep is built chiefly of Bargate stone from the Godalming area. This was a royal castle, much visited before the 15th century by the monarchs and their families, but afterwards falling into decay. The keep alone was kept in repair because it was used as a prison until the 16th century. The castle precincts originally contained many other buildings of which nothing remains.

From *Access for the Disabled*

⟫ Test it ⟩⟩⟩

Use these three extracts to write five paragraphs suggesting how a family could spend a day by the river at Guildford on 10 August. Include details of activities.

Dapdune Wharf, Wharf Road, Guildford GU1 4RR
Tel 01483 561389 *Fax* 01483 531667
Email riverwey@ntrust.org.uk
www.nationaltrust.org.uk/riverwey

- explore inside 'Reliance', a restored Wey barge, to see the cargo and cabin - and hear from the 'Captain'
- interactive exhibition, including models, telling the story of the waterway, how the barges were built and the people who lived and worked there

- enjoy a picnic with the family on Dapdune 'Island'
- river trips
- hands-on discovery room in the Old Gunpowder Store
- join the fun as the Wey Navigation celebrates its 350th anniversary

Opening Times & Information

Wharf	22 Mar - 2 Nov	11 - 5	**M** T **W** T **F S S**

Notes: River trips 11–4 (conditions permitting). Access to towpath during daylight hours all year

→ ½ml N of Guildford town centre on the River Wey, just off A322, (Woodbridge Road) behind Surrey Cricket Ground
🚌 28 Guildford – Woking, 20 Guildford – Aldershot, 4 Guildford – Park Barn (cricket ground, 100 yards)
♿ **Wharf** Wheelchair access with care
💷 £3

🚶 **THE WILD WEY**
Sun 10 Aug, 2.30pm at Pyrford Lock
A five-mile walk along the towpath looking at the rich variety of wildlife living in and around the waterway. £1 charge.

 PAPER PLAY ACTIVITY DAY
Thurs 7 August, Dapdune Wharf
Have a go at making your own paper following in the footsteps of a navigation tradition. £1 charge.

GUILDFORD BOAT HOUSE
Public River Trips on board
The Harry Stevens
2003

Time	Departure Point	Description	Arrival Point	Time
Departs 1.45pm	Town Wharf Guildford	1 1/2 hour cruise upstream to St Catherine's and return to Guildford Boat House (picking up at Guildford Boat House en route)	Guildford Boat House	Arrives 3.15pm
Departs 2.15pm	Guildford Boat House	¾ hour return trip - Pick up point for cruise above	Guildford Boat House	Arrives 3.15pm
Departs 3.30pm	Guildford Boat House	¾ hour return trip to St Catherine's Lock	Guildford Boat House	Arrives 4.15pm

Days Trips Run
Saturday 12 April to Friday 18 July 2003
Trips run every Saturday and Sunday and from 7 May every Wednesday afternoons, plus Bank Holiday Mondays
Saturday 19 July to Sunday 7 September 2003
Trips run everyday except Monday and Friday (ie Sun, Tue, Wed, Thu, Sat) plus Bank Holiday Monday
Monday 8 September to Sunday 12 October 2003
Saturday, Sunday, Wednesday
There no trips on Mondays (except Bank Holiday Mondays) or Fridays

Prices
Short trips from Guildford Boat House
Adult £3.00 Child (5-12years) £1.75
1 1/2 hour trips
Adult £5.00 Child (5-12years) £2.50
Children under 5 free, but must be declared for safety reasons
no pre booking - please pay on board

What you get marks for

Including suitable and accurate information for the family	1 mark
Creating a new coherent format	2 marks
Using a consistent style	3 marks
Using language suitable for a family looking for a fun day out	2 marks
It looks like a useful leaflet that really would help a family to plan their day	2 marks
Total	**10 marks**

8. Drafting at the computer

In this masterclass you will learn how to:

- choose a planning strategy
- make best use of your word processor to write and present work
- redraft and check work on screen.

Choosing a planning strategy

Before you start on your writing, stop and think where to begin.

Yes, start on the writing if:

- you already know what you want to say
- you already know how you will organise the writing.

But wait a moment if:

- your thoughts are still jumbled and incomplete
- there isn't an obvious order
- you know how to start but not how to end.

A lot of non-fiction writing is easier to plan as a diagram:

A grid

	Feature 1	Feature 2	Feature 3
Subject 1			
Subject 2			
Subject 3			

Star chart

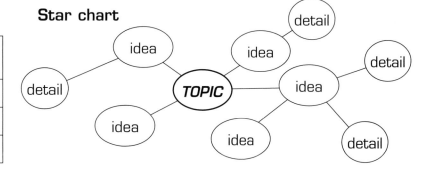

Activity 1: Planning

Which planning diagram would you use for:

- discussion of a controversial topic?
- a review of different careers?
- explaining how to apply for a bank loan?
- things to think about before buying a car?

A flow chart

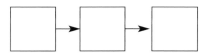

For and against columns

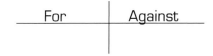

Drafting using a word processor

Here is a good basic drafting strategy:

1 Gather and plan your ideas.
– Follow the advice in Masterclass 5.

2 List the sections on the screen.
– These act as guides even if you want to delete them later.

3 Write the opening sentence of each section.
– This will give you a structure and a feel for the style.

4 Write one or two paragraphs in each section.
– If you find this hard, start with a section you feel confident about.

5 Print out your work and read it back for the overall effect. Mark in changes.
– Check the content, structure, order, style and links between sections.

6 Make any big changes to content and organisation.
– This may mean adding things in, cutting things out, changing the order or rewording key sentences.

7 On screen, read each paragraph and improve the expression.
– This means listening for false notes, getting the style right, and making it clear. Correct spelling errors.

8 On screen, apply any layout features.
– This means boldface, colour, use of boxes, shapes, etc.

9 Print out and do a final check.
– Make last-minute changes with a red pen.

10 Correct on screen.

Activity 2: Introduction to the school play

Here is a plan for the introduction to a school play, *In and Out of Trouble,* which will appear in the programme.

Introduction to *In and Out of Trouble*:

1 Welcome – main things to celebrate.
2 About the play itself.
3 What it is about, its themes.
4 About the production of the play in school.
5 Thanks to various people.

- Write the first sentence only of each paragraph.
- Write a quick first full draft of paragraphs 3 and 4 on a word processor. Make up the details.
- Swap with someone else, then improve the draft starting at point 5 in the drafting process on the opposite page.
- Discuss what you find most difficult about improving drafts and find out how others tackle these difficulties.

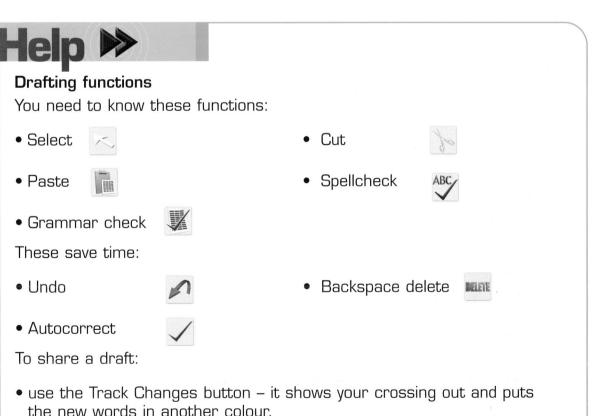

Help ▶▶

Drafting functions

You need to know these functions:

- Select
- Paste
- Grammar check

These save time:

- Undo
- Autocorrect

- Cut
- Spellcheck

- Backspace delete

To share a draft:

- use the Track Changes button – it shows your crossing out and puts the new words in another colour.

Find out if you have any planning aids on your computer.

Using the layout toolkit

You need to know these functions:

For the words:

- boldface
- underline
- font size

- italics
- font style

For line layout:

- spacing
- justifying
- centring and flushing right or left

- bullets
- indenting

For shape on the page:

- boxes
- columns

- borders
- margins

For decoration and illustration:

- clip art
- shapes
- colour fill

- word art
- colour

Activity 3: Tiger Lil's card

How many layout features can you spot in this folded pocket-size card?

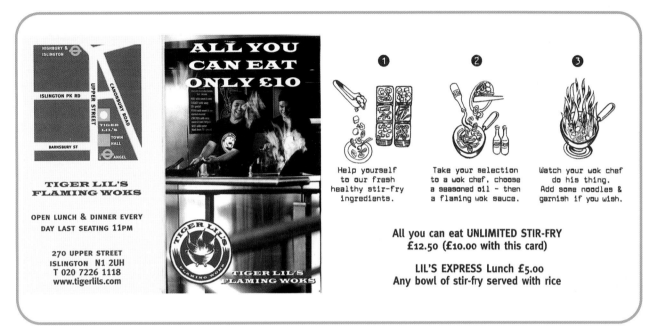

Activity 4: Layout

1   Write the following text into your word processor and apply all the layout functions to make it eye-catching and easier to read:

**West Lake Summer Sunshine Music Festival featuring
tribute bands New Abba The Beetles and Nice Girls.
Saturday 28 July at Lakeside Arena. 7pm BBQ and bar 8pm
Disco 9pm Bands 11pm Disco 12am Fireworks. Tickets £12
from Civic Hall or Lakeside box office. Sponsored by
Lakeside Radio – your local station rocking for you on 96.4.**

2   Afterwards, compare results and discuss which of the features make it too cluttered and overpowering and should be used less often.

3   Discuss what should guide you in choosing which features to use.

Choosing layout features
- Base your design on the main information.
- Keep it simple and bold.
- Clear space is more useful than lots of fancy layout.

Design the back of a new breakfast cereal packet. Convince your readers that the new cereal is really good for them. You can make up the details.

1 Do a plan.
2 Draft the words.
3 Apply layout.

What you get marks for

For the plan

The plan clearly shows the main sections of content	1 mark
The plan clearly shows the main elements of layout	1 mark

For the draft of words

Several keywords or headings are in place	1 mark
The style is upbeat and persuasive	1 mark
The information is varied and interesting	1 mark
The writing is broken into short, readable sections	1 mark

For the layout

The layout is attractively laid out in short, readable sections	1 mark
The main messages about the benefits of the cereal are easy to pick out	2 marks
The presentation is cheerful and upbeat to start the day well	1 mark
Total	**10 marks**

9. Enriching your sentences

In this masterclass you will learn how to:

- start and finish sentences in a number of different ways
- add extra details into and onto sentences
- draw the reader in to the detail.

Different ways to start a sentence

Escape repetition by using different openings. For example:

Start by saying *when* it happened:

> **Later that night, Jenny's father walked her home.**

Start by saying *where* it happened:

> **At the corner of York Lane, they were surprised by a thief who snatched her bag.**

Start by saying *why* it happened:

> **To prevent his escape, Jenny hooked her foot around his leg causing him to trip.**

Start by saying *how* it happened:

> **Without a moment's hesitation, her dad grabbed Jenny's bag and hurried Jenny home.**

Start with an *-ing* or an *-ly* or an *-ed:*

> **Unwilling to be beaten, the thief followed them.**
> **Luckily, they were not far from their own front door.**
> **Relieved to be safely home, Jenny and her dad called the police.**

Notice that all these openers are followed by a comma that separates them from the main sentence.

Different ways to end a sentence

End with a *fact*:

> **Two hundred years ago, *it was rare to have a toilet of your own in a house*.**

End with a *repetition*:

> **Today we take it for granted that each house will have its own toilet, and the idea of managing without one is unacceptable, *unthinkable*.**

End with an *action*:

> **I found this out as a student when I took a room in a rented house that was rather tatty. When I moved in, the landlord *promised to redecorate*.**

End with a *detail*:

> **The decorator was fond of talking about politics and spent much of his day lecturing his assistant, *who nodded wisely but said little*.**

> **One day I returned home to find water cascading down the stairs, and the cistern was lying in broken pieces around the bathroom floor, *its splinters swimming in a pool of water*.**

End with a *surprise*:

> **'You fool!' the decorator was yelling to his assistant. '*I said "Smash the system," not the "Cistern"!*'**

Activity 1: Easter bonnet

Use a range of different sentence openings and endings to write a
short anecdote in five sentences based on this cartoon:

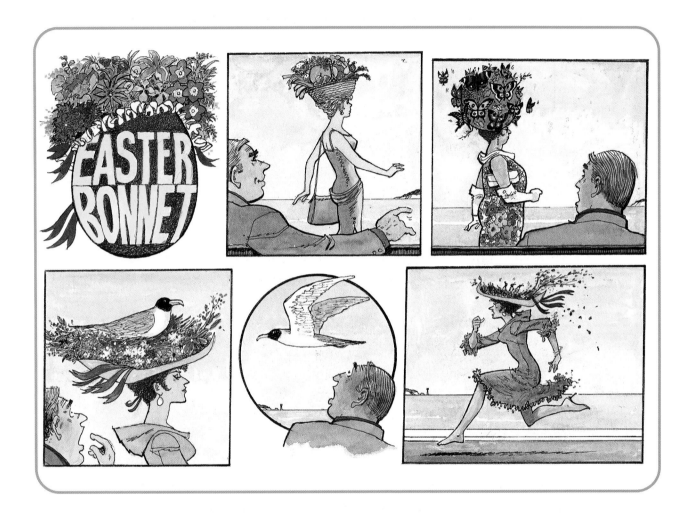

Adding on detail

Many writers pull the reader deeper into the story by extending sentences with intriguing details. The details make it real for the reader, and capture the imagination.

An example:

> The fields all round her house were shrouded in snow, with patches of dark earth poking through here and there as if the world were a rich fruit cake under cream.

From *Under the Skin* by Michel Faber

This sentence is extended twice: the first time to look closer (*with patches of dark earth poking through here and there*), and the second time to make it sharp and real (*as if the world were a rich fruit cake under cream*). This is an image with colour and taste. It turns a familiar scene into something special.

Activity 2: Adding on details

Use the same sort of extensions on the next sentences in the story:

> In the western field, tiny golden sheep stood marooned in the whiteness, XXXXXXXXXXXXXXXXXXXXXXXXXXXXXX.
>
> In the northern field, XXXXXXXXXXXXXXXXXXXXXXX.

Fill them in with details that will capture the imagination and make it real for the reader. Then compare them with the writer's original sentences at the end of this masterclass.

Listing details

Another way of extending sentences is to cluster details at the end.
For example:

> The fields were all rented out to various local landowners, who would bring along what was needed at ploughing times, harvesting time, lambing time and so on. In between times, the land lay silent and untouched, and the farm building rotted, rusted and grew moss.

From *Under the Skin* by **Michel Faber**

The number of details makes a difference:

- Two things in a list sound like nothing else matters.
- Three things in a list sounds like a selection from many details.
- Four or more things in a list sounds like a full list.

Dropping in details

Writers also grab attention by dropping details into the middle of a sentence.

> **Fifteen minutes later, perspiring, shivering a little, she padded over to the wardrobe and selected her clothes for the day, the same clothes as yesterday.**

- This sentence has a starter in front of it: *Fifteen minutes later.*
- It also has a detail added to the end: *the same clothes as yesterday.*
- And it also details dropped in the middle: *perspiring, shivering a little.*

Activity 3: Dropping in details

Try dropping details into the middle of these sentences:

> **Holly struggled on under the weight of her backpack. She now regretted her decision to bring extra clothes.**

⏩ Test it ⟩⟩⟩

Here are some bare sentences. Expand them by adding on or dropping in details to make them richer. Then add two sentences to the end to bring it to a conclusion.

> Isserley's eyes were sore.
> She blinked until the lids stayed shut.
> She would rest her eyes for just a little while.
> There was a spot she knew off the main road.
> Nobody ever went there.
> It was just the place for Isserley.
> Isserley fell asleep.
> She dreamed at first of ruins.
> Then she slipped into a deeper dream.

Clauses taken from *Under the Skin* by Michel Faber

What you get marks for

Half a mark for expanding each sentence with starters, add-ons or add-ins	up to 4.5 marks
For at least three striking effective details	3 marks
For overall effect and fluency	2.5 marks
Total	**10 marks**

ANSWERS

In the western field, tiny golden sheep stood marooned in the whiteness, *shoving their faces into the snow in search of buried sweetness.*

In the northern field, *a giant mound of turnips on a raft of hay shone like frosted cherries in the sun.*

10. *Shifting your focus*

In this masterclass you will learn how to:

- shift from focus to focus when you write
- shift between different times and places
- shift perspective.

When you think, you hop from idea to idea, one thought setting off another. Some ideas come to nothing, and others you develop. Your thoughts are always shifting focus.

Writing is similar: it moves from focus to focus. Each sentence is a thought. The shifts from sentence to sentence mimic the chain of thoughts in the mind.

You already know that you should start a new paragraph when you change topic, time, place or perspective. But there are smaller shifts from sentence to sentence, as the camera eye of the writer moves between thoughts.

From sentence to sentence, you can shift focus:

- from one place to another
- from one event to another
- from one time to another
- from one person to another
- from one detail to another
- from one topic to another
- from one perspective to another.

Shifting focus from place to place

Shifting focus from place to place in writing mimics what happens as we look around.

Activity 1: Camera eye

Try this now. Look around the place you are in. Notice the way your eye tends to focus on one thing, or one spot, at a time.

Here is a written example. In this extract, the narrator remembers that, as a child, he and his friend had a den in the bushes. Notice how the focus shifts, like a camera looking in different places:

> If you know the right spot, in the shrubs that were once the front hedge of Braemar, you can part the screen of vegetation and crawl along a kind of low passageway under the branches into a secret chamber that we've hacked out in the very heart of the thicket. Its floor is bare, hardened earth. A green twilight filters through the leaves. Even when it rains it hardly penetrates this far. When we're in here no-one in the world can see us.

From *Spies* by Michael Frayn

If this were made into a film, it would be easy to pick the camera shots because the writer moves focus from place to place, taking you step by step into the den and looking round.

Activity 2: Describe the classroom

Write a paragraph describing your classroom.

Help ▶▶

Structuring descriptions of place

Descriptions of place shift focus as the eye would, moving from spot to spot to take in the whole. The trick is to decide how to sequence them in an order that makes sense, e.g. from nearby to further away, from front to back. Try one of these approaches:

- Set the scene and then hop from person to person.
- Set the scene and then hop from place to place: up at the front; the pupils near the door; the pupils at the back, etc.
- Start with yourself, then move to the people near you, then the people further away.

Shifting focus from time to time

The most common shift in stories is the shift through time. This is because stories are usually told in order of events.

Activity 3: Shifts in time

1   In this paragraph, the same writer describes the same den by shifting in time. Spot the shifts.

Afterwards, turn to the end of this masterclass for an explanation.

> Two summers ago this was our camp, where we plotted various expeditions into the African jungle and took refuge from the Royal Canadian Mounted Police. Last summer it was our hide, where we did our birdwatching. Now it's to be the headquarters of a much more serious enterprise.

From *Spies* by Michael Frayn

2   Pick an event at school and describe it in three shifts like the paragraph above, e.g. sports day, detention, or an examination.

Shifting focus in other ways

Shifts in time and place are very common in stories, but they are not the only ways to move between ideas.

Activity 4: Different kinds of shift

How do these two extracts shift focus? Afterwards, find the answers at the end of this masterclass.

> I see the cottages, the sly tumbledown hovels lurking behind the undergrowth in a debris of rusty oil drums and broken prams. I hear the barking of the misshapen dogs that rushed out at us as we passed, and I feel the sullen gaze of the raggedy children who watched us from behind their wicket gates. I smell the sour, catty stink of the trees around the collapsed and abandoned farm.

> I wait, scarcely daring to breathe. On the opposite pavement the Geest twins are chalking out a hopscotch diagram, and Norman Stott is rubbing it out with the sole of his shoe. Barbara Berrill walks past, calling to the Stotts' dog. At any moment one of the children is going to hear.

From *Spies* by Michael Frayn

Shifting perspective

Writers sometimes shift perspective. For example:

- from one narrator to another
- from one angle to another
- from one point of view to another.

Activity 5: Shift of perspective

In this extract, the narrator is an old man who has returned to the street where he lived as a boy. Notice the shifts between the sentences.

> **Going back**
>
> I walk slowly up to the little turning circle at the end. The same fourteen houses sit calmly complacent in the warm, dull summer afternoon, exactly as they always did. I walk slowly back to the corner again. It's all still here, exactly as it always was. I don't know why I should find this so surprising. I wasn't expecting anything different. And yet, after fifty years…
>
> **From *Spies* by Michael Frayn**

1. The sentences alternate in the way they are expressed. Can you see how?
2. Can you think *why*?
3. Afterwards, turn to the end of this masterclass for an explanation.

The prevailing first person

Writing in the first person means writing as *I*. But this does not mean that every sentence must begin with I. If you start a paragraph with I and most of the sentences use I, then it is possible to slip out of it for short periods and your reader will understand that the story is still being told from this perspective. Readers accept the prevailing voice as long as the breaks from it are short. For example:

> **I hold the key in my hand. *It is cold, smooth and heavy.* I turn it over and over and wonder what it opens.**

The first and last sentence are told in the first person (*I*), but the middle sentence is written in the third person (*he, she* or *it*) about the key. Nonetheless, you understand when you read it that *cold, smooth and heavy* is how it feels to the narrator.

Activity 6: Shifts in and out of a first person narrative

1 Read this extract and mark where it drops in and out of the first person as the focus shifts:

Digging up a secret box at midnight

I strain my ears. Nothing. Just the shifting of the leaves, the sigh of the wires, the coming and going of my breath…

I focus my attention back on the contents of the box. The underside of it feels the same as the top. It's about as wide as my hand… Yes I know what this is. I begin to slide my hand along it so I can feel the end of it to check, then stop again.

The sound that's changed, I realise, is the sound of my breathing. It's grown more complex. It no longer corresponds precisely to the rise and fall I can feel inside my chest.

I stop breathing. The sound of breathing continues.

There's someone a few feet away in the lane – someone who has come silently up to the gap in the wire fence and then stopped to listen, as I'm listening now.

From *Spies* by Michael Frayn

2 Work out why the writer drops out of the first person at certain points, and then returns to it.

3 Once you have discussed this, turn to the end of this masterclass for an explanation.

4 Continue the story in the first person for one or two paragraphs. Will you open the box? What will you do about the other person? Drop out of the first person once or twice to 'see' or 'hear' things going on around you.

▶▶ Test it))))

Write three paragraphs of at least three sentences each from the middle of a story in which you and two friends have to get back a secret message which has been confiscated by the teacher who has it, unread, in her desk drawer. Make full use of the shifting eye.

Paragraph 1 – Draw straws to decide who goes to get it back.

Paragraph 2 – Watch for your moment.

Paragraph 3 – Get it.

What you get marks for

In paragraph 1, for shifting the focus between people	3 marks
In paragraph 2, for shifting the focus between places/objects	3 marks
In paragraph 3, for shifting focus between first person and third person perspectives	3 marks
For overall effect	1 mark
Total	**10 marks**

ANSWERS

Shifting focus (The den)
The focus shifts over time, from two years ago, to one year ago, then up to the time of the story.

Different kinds of shift
The first extract shifts from sense to sense (sight, hearing, smell). The second extract shifts from person to person.

Alternating sentences (Going back)
The sentences alternate between the first person I and what he sees (*The same fourteen houses, It's all still here*). He looks and then he tell us what he sees. It recreates the experience of him looking and trying to digest, after all these years, what he sees. It's as though his eyes and his brain are having a conversation.

Alternating sentences (Secret box)
The sentences are expressed in the first person when he is absorbed in what he is doing, but switch to the third person when he becomes more aware of the other things around him, and the focus moves onto them. The writer is communicating where the boy is directing his attention.

IMPROVING YOUR STYLE

11. Improving the flow of your sentences

In this masterclass you will learn how to:

- understand the value of connectives
- link ideas together
- make the reader make the links between ideas.

Connectives

Some types of writing – such as explanations, instructions and arguments – depend on clear links between ideas which help the reader to follow the points. The easiest way to link ideas together is to use a joining word or phrase: a connective.

Activity 1: Sorting connectives

Here are eight headings. Match an equal number of connectives to each one. Find the answers at the end of the masterclass.

Types

Shifting in time	Shifting point of view	Comparing	Reasoning or logic
Adding to	Qualifying	Exemplifying	Summarising

Connectives

For example	Therefore	Immediately	Overall
In addition	Similarly	Although	For instance
Later	Inevitably	Afterwards	Taken as a whole
Alternatively	If only	In the same way	Furthermore
On the other hand	Moreover	In short	As a result
On the contrary	Likewise	Unless	In the case of

Making links

Activity 2: Without links

The links have been removed from this paragraph. Try reading it:

The earliest settlers in the Nile valley in Egypt lived in small villages. The valley was narrow. The villages were packed closely together. There were often quarrels between them. They quarrelled about water rights. They quarrelled about which village should farm a particular piece of land. The leader of one village in a particular district gained control over many neighbouring villages. The local chieftain settled all disputes. The local chieftain controlled irrigation trenches and canals. The local chieftain defended the area. The local chieftain acted as chief priest to the local god.

- What is difficult about reading unlinked sentences?
- How could it be made clearer and easier to read?
- Rewrite it to be clear and easy.
- Name the techniques you used to make it clear and fluent.
- Afterwards, compare your answers with those used by the original writer at the end of the masterclass.

Links

There are many ways to link ideas:

- List them together in one sentence.
- Use a link word (a **conjunction**) to join them together, e.g. *and, because, but.*
- Use a connecting phrase (a **connective**) to spell out the link, e.g. *as a result of, later that day.*
- Repeat or 'echo' key words (or words similar to them) in the next sentence so the reader realises you are still on the same subject.
- Instead of repeating names, use pronouns (John... his... he... him...).
- Use a string of links, e.g. *firstly, secondly, thirdly; One reason is... Another reason is... A further reason is...*

Activity 3: Connectives

1   Identify the connectives in this paragraph and say what kind of links they are.

> Most of Modern Egypt is a barren desert. The only part which is not desert is the Nile Valley. Because hardly any rain falls in Egypt, the Nile valley too would be desert if it were not for the summer rains of the Abyssinian mountains. These cause the river to flood every year, so that from mid-August to October, most of the valley is under water. When the flood subsides, it leaves behind a thin layer of black mud, or silt, which is very fertile.

From *Out of the Ancient World* by Victor Skipp

Find the answers at the end of the masterclass.

2   Here is the same paragraph without links. What is the effect?

> Most of Modern Egypt is a barren desert. The Nile valley is not a desert. Hardly any rain falls in Egypt. The rain falls in summer on the Abyssinian mountains. The river floods every year. From mid-August to October, most of the valley is under water. The flood subsides. A thin layer of black mud, or silt, is very fertile.

3   Could you link the ideas together in a way that is different from that used by the writer? Try it. You could do this orally instead of in writing.

Making the reader make the links

Not every kind of writing needs bold links. Some writers like to make their readers work at it:

> The motorway roared silently. Birds skittered the water in flight to more distant reeds, and the iron water lay again, flat light reflecting no sky. The caravans and the birches. Tom.
>
> 'Next week,' said Jan. 'Right?' Her knuckles were comfortless between his. 'Next week. I go next week.' She tried to reach the pain, but his eyes would not let her in.
>
> 'London?'
>
> 'Yes.'

From *Red Shift* by Alan Garner

The writer leaves out the help we usually expect:

- clues about who is speaking
- a narrator who explains things.

In fact, you can avoid connectives altogether by using a semicolon instead.

The right way to use a semicolon

The semicolon joins two clauses (simple sentences) together to signal that they are closely linked, but without saying how. For example:

Evening fell and night settled on the battlefield; Patrus yawned and laid back his head.

The reader has to make the link between the late hour and Patrus feeling sleepy.

Activity 4: Semicolons

1 Suggest the implied link in:

> **Patrus' sword gleamed with Malco's blood; he savoured the taste of victory.**

> **Malco's body lay cold under the moonlight; even when the other bodies were removed, his remained undisturbed.**

2 Replace the connectives with semicolons in these sentences, rewording as necessary, and then judge the effect.

> **Patrus looked down at the body of Malco, *causing* a pang of guilt to pass through him.**

> **He wondered if everyone felt this way after battle, *but he deduced from* the sounds of celebration around the camp fire that they did not.**

The right way to use a colon

The colon (:) acts like an equal sign (=) in mathematics. It means 'to put it another way'. It holds two halves of a sentence in balance, one half equal to the other. Sometimes, one half summarises the other. The other half unpacks the summary.

> **He remembered the life he had before he joined the Roman army: he had his family; his small farm; friends in the village; the well and the pool beneath the trees; his sister and her family on the next farm and his parents only half a day's walk away in the hills.**

> **That was the moment that Patrus decided that he would never fight again: he would put away his armour, hang up his sword and return home.**

You could quite easily put a full stop where a colon goes and start a new sentence, but the colon prompts the reader to make the link.

▶▶ Test it))

Use this diagram to explain in writing only (no diagrams) what is inside the Great Pyramid of Cheops in Egypt.
Write three paragraphs:

Paragraph 1 – An overview of the pyramid and what it is for.

Paragraph 2 – About the chambers inside.

Paragraph 3 – How it was made.

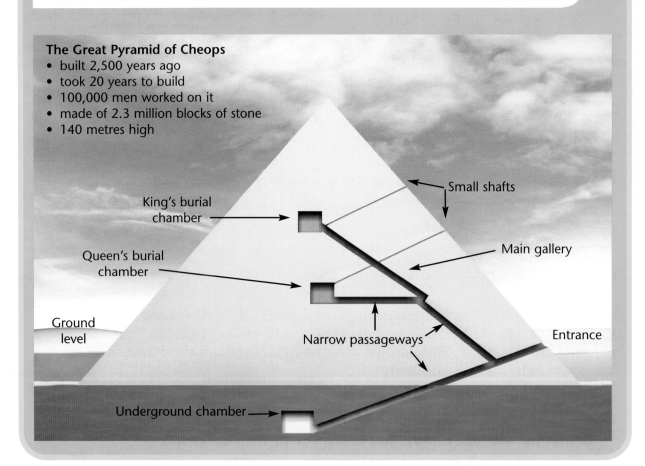

The Great Pyramid of Cheops
- built 2,500 years ago
- took 20 years to build
- 100,000 men worked on it
- made of 2.3 million blocks of stone
- 140 metres high

King's burial chamber

Queen's burial chamber

Small shafts

Main gallery

Ground level

Narrow passageways

Entrance

Underground chamber

What you get marks for

Connectives have often been used to link information together	3 marks
Similar facts have been combined together into single sentences	3 marks
Ways have been found to link other ideas together, e.g. by repeating key words	2 marks
The overall effect sounds fluent	2 marks
Total	**10 marks**

ANSWERS

Sorting connectives

Shifting in time
Immediately
Later
Afterwards

Reasoning or logic
Therefore
Inevitably
As a result

Exemplifying
For example
For instance
In the case of

Shifting point of view
Alternatively
On the other hand
On the contrary

Adding to
In addition
Furthermore
Moreover

Summarising
Overall
Taken as a whole
In short

Comparing
Similarly
In the same way
Likewise

Qualifying
Although
If only
Unless

The original passage in Activity 2

The earliest settlers in the Nile valley in Egypt lived in small villages. Because of the narrowness of the valley, the villages were packed closely together, and there were often quarrels between them, about such things as water rights, and which village should farm a particular piece of land. Eventually, the leader of one village in a particular district gained control over many neighbouring villages. From then onwards, this local chieftain settled all disputes. He also controlled the irrigation trenches and canals, defended the area and acted as chief priest to the local god.

From *Out of the Ancient World* by Victor Skipp

The original passage in Activity 3

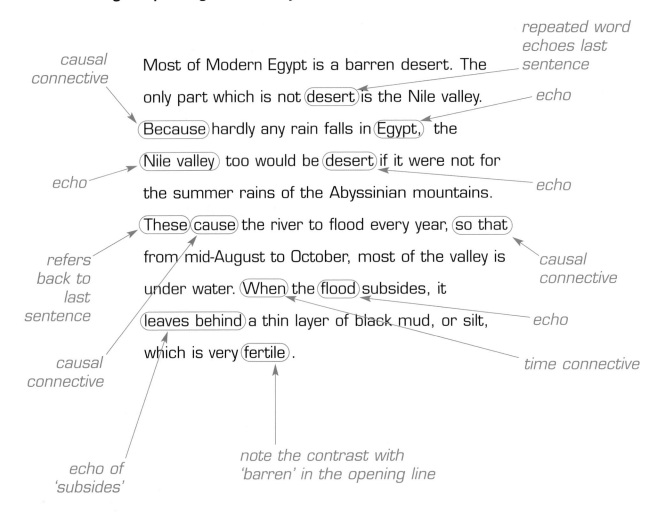

causal connective

repeated word echoes last sentence

Most of Modern Egypt is a barren desert. The only part which is not desert is the Nile valley. Because hardly any rain falls in Egypt, the Nile valley too would be desert if it were not for the summer rains of the Abyssinian mountains. These cause the river to flood every year, so that from mid-August to October, most of the valley is under water. When the flood subsides, it leaves behind a thin layer of black mud, or silt, which is very fertile.

echo

echo

echo

refers back to last sentence

causal connective

causal connective

echo

time connective

echo of 'subsides'

note the contrast with 'barren' in the opening line

12. Writing longer sentences

In this masterclass you will learn how to:

- shape your sentences to fit your meaning
- build longer, more sophisticated sentences
- use commas correctly.

Shaping sentences to fit your meaning

Longer sentences are more easily shaped to fit your meaning.

Activity 1: Sentence organisation

1 How are the sentences in this paragraph constructed to reflect the content?

Napoleon invades Russia

The Russians steadily retreated, burning their crops and drawing Napoleon's army deeper into Russia and further from its supplies. Napoleon reached Moscow, which the Russians abandoned and burnt. Still the Russians refused to make peace, and Napoleon saw that he had to retreat. His army was now caught by the bitter Russian winter, and his frozen and starving men died in their thousands.

From *The Oxford Children's Encyclopaedia*

2 Rewrite these sentences so that their shapes reflect their meanings:

A Greek man called Euclid wrote a school textbook called *Elements of Geometry* over 2000 years ago. Today's textbooks are still based on it and some people call it 'the most studied book apart from the Bible'. Most of his other books have been lost. That's all we know about Euclid.

Building longer sentences

There are several ways to combine ideas in sentences.

The Arctic is a land of ice and snow.
It lies on the roof of the world.
In winter, the days shorten until it is night
all the time.
The night sky is filled with the shimmering
Northern Lights.

Method 1: Hitching

You can hitch them together with simple joining words:

The Arctic is a land of ice and snow *which* lies on the roof of
the world *where*, in winter, the days shorten until it is night
all the time *and* the night sky is filled with the shimmering
Northern Lights.

Advantages: It's easy – just drop in the links.

Disadvantages: It sounds clunky and simplistic.

Method 2: Merging

You can move the parts around so that one of them is the main sentence and the others are placed before, after and inside it as add-ons, drop-ins and asides.

At the roof of the world lies the Arctic, a land of ice and
snow where the Northern Lights shimmer in the sky as the
long winter night descends.

The frozen Arctic lies at the roof of the world, beneath the
shimmering Northern Lights that illuminate the long winter
night.

Advantages: It sounds whole and sophisticated.

Disadvantages: You have to be bold to cut out words, move parts around and edit them together.

Help ▶▶

Merging ideas together

Try some of these techniques:

- Remove repetition (e.g. of the word *night*).
- Shorten where there is more detail than you need.
- Pack some of the information into adjectives or adverbs (*The* frozen *Arctic*).
- Feel free to move ideas around and re-express them.
- Say the main thing first, then add the rest on as extra detail.
- Use shorter links (*the* long *winter night*).
- Hold on to distinctive wording (e.g. *lies at the roof of the world*).

Activity 2: Merging sentences

Collapse these three lists of ideas into single well-shaped sentences:

1   Eggs

Fish lay eggs in water.
Turtles lay eggs.
Crocodiles lay eggs.
Birds lay eggs.
Most land eggs are covered in a hard shell.
The shell protects the baby creature inside.
The yellow yolk contains the baby.
The yolk floats safely in the albumen or white of the egg.

2   Cork

Corks are made from the bark of young cork oak trees.
Cork oak trees grow in the Mediterranean.
The cork is cut from the tree when it is about 15 years old.
Cork is cut from the tree every ten years.
Each tree lives for approximately 150 years.

3   Feathers

All birds have feathers.
Feathers grow out of the bird's skin, in the same way that human
skin grows hair and nails.
Feathers are light.
Feathers have no feeling.
Feathers make a waterproof covering for the bird.
Feathers – especially fluffy feathers – keep birds warm.
Feathers on the wing help birds to fly in air.
Not all birds fly.

The correct use of the comma

There are three ways to use commas:

1. To separate items or actions in a list

Girls hate sarcasm, criticism, ridicule and being ignored.

- The last two items do not need a comma because they are joined by the word *and*.

2. To separate speech from the rest of the sentence

'I despise sarcasm,' declared Jenny.

'So unlike you to do that,' sneered Jack.

'Do stop squabbling,' pleaded Jane, 'and let's get started.'

- The comma always comes before the speech marks.
- The comma replaces the usual full stop because it is not at the end of the sentence.
- The comma is not needed if there is a *?* or a *!*

3. To chunk longer sentences by separating the main clause from the rest

The **main clause** of the following sentence is *Ahmed woke instantly at six o'clock*. You can tell it is the main clause because it can stand alone and still makes sense without the rest of the sentence.

Just as he did every morning, Ahmed woke instantly at six o'clock, convinced he had forgotten something.

The clauses that go before and after it are **subordinate clauses**. They add something to the main clause, but they would not make sense alone. They are dependent on the main clause for their meaning.

Commas are placed between the main clause and the others for two good reasons:

- to help the reader to spot the main clause
- to break up a long sentence into helpful chunks of meaning.

Commas

- Commas are not pauses, but they often signal a change of tone, like a car changing gear. Read a sentence aloud and see if you can hear it.

- Modern punctuation tends to leave out commas if it can be done without harming the meaning.

- The 'comma splice' is the most common error with commas. It happens when commas are used to string together short expressions one after another instead of using full stops. It sometimes happens by mistake when several sentences start with the same pronoun.

Activity 3: Commas

Insert one list comma and four clause commas into this paragraph.

Cheer yourself up by changing your room. For a start you can move the furniture around for an instant change. Next pick up some cardboard boxes from the supermarket and paint them with bold colours. Sort your stuff into the boxes throwing out what you don't use any more. Put up a noticeboard stick up a new poster and hang a mobile perhaps a glitter ball.

Find the answers at the end of the masterclass.

⏩ Test it ⟩⟩⟩

Use the information to write a short article about the first astronaut.

The first astronaut

Yuri Gagarin

born 1934 in Russia

parents were poor farmers

first job – steelworker

flying was his hobby

joined air force

space race between Russians and Americans

animals had been sent on test flights

first manned space mission – 12 April 1961

spaceship *Vostok* circled the Earth for less than two hours

he became a hero, everyone wanted to meet him

he travelled to many countries, crowds cheered him

died 1968 aged 34 testing a new aeroplane

buried in wall of Kremlin in Moscow

Americans landed a man on Moon in July 1969

What you get marks for

For combining information sensibly into longer sentences	3 marks
For using commas correctly to chunk up sentences	3 marks
For achieving a sophisticated style	4 marks
Total	**10 marks**

ANSWERS

Commas

- A list comma after *noticeboard*.
- Clause commas after *start*, *Next*, *boxes* and *mobile*.

13. Inform, explain, describe

In this masterclass you will learn how to:

- present information so it is easy to use
- explain complicated processes with clarity
- describe things that are not so easy to visualise.

Presenting information so it is easy to use

Sometimes information is read for pleasure and entertainment, like a story. The writer has time to dwell on the interesting things. Information of this sort is usually written in full sentences and paragraphs.

At other times, information is there for reference so it must be quick and easy to use. In this case it has boxes, headings, bullet points and diagrams. Sentences are short so the reader can get at the information quickly.

Activity 1: The Mystery Spot

1   Fold an A4 sheet into three and cut out one section to use. Use one side only.

2   Read the information on the next two pages about a place in California known as *The Mystery Spot*.

3   Your task is to write a handy tourist leaflet telling people what the Mystery Spot is and what they need to know to make a visit.

Help ▶▶

At-a-glance information

- Categorise the information and present it in separate sections.
- Use sub-headings.
- Use space, layout and boxes to divide up the sections.
- Cut out what you don't need.
- Use bullet points.
- Use visual aids: maps, grids, arrows, diagrams.

1

The Mystery Spot is a 150 square foot piece of hillside land in the Santa Cruz redwoods, where, it is said, a compass will not work, and where people appear to grow and shrink. It opened to the public in 1939, and not much has changed since then except tours went from a nickel to five dollars. In summer, a thousand people a day make the pilgrimage here from all over the world. What brings them? Mostly curiosity. Claims are that gravity doesn't apply here, balls roll uphill, and people appear to lean at odd angles to the earth.

From *www.savvytraveler.org*

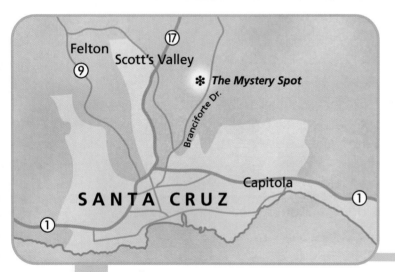

2

Recently discovered is a spot, 150 feet in diameter, located in the redwoods of the Santa Cruz Mountains of California. The visitor to this Mystery Spot leans towards the southwest upon entering the area, and the lean becomes more acute as he proceeds towards the centre of the spot. Even the trees here do not stand perpendicular.

The sensational Mystery Spot is a series of surprises that are unique, different, inexplicable. It is not like anything else I ever saw or heard of and I have seen most of the noted places in California and many other states.

It appears as though every law of gravitation has gone haywire, turned topsy-turvy and just doesn't make sense. Some unseen magnetism or phenomenon just upsets all former ideas of equilibrium. What is it that makes one stand up leaning backwards or sideways?

From *www.mysteryspot.com*

3

Two parallel cement blocks about four feet long are embedded in the asphalt path. In the centre sits a carpenter's level with the bead centred exactly. Our guide, Randall, stands at one end, Joe at the other. Joe is about a foot taller than Randall. Then they trade sides. Joe appears to have shrunk, although both men are standing on a level surface. In 1948, the cover of *Life* magazine showed a smiling couple standing at this very spot, demonstrating this shrink and grow phenomenon. As a short person, I find the idea of instantly gaining height very appealing.

A short, steep climb brings us to the famous tilting cabin. Its door, walls and floor all slant at impossible angles. Inside the cabin, our guide climbs onto a narrow shelf suspended about four feet from the steeply canted floor. He appears to be leaning out from the ledge at a 17–degree angle into thin air.

This place might be a hoax, but there's nothing fake about my car sick feeling. The odd angles are confusing my sense of equilibrium. OK, so most of this is optical illusion. But what explains the other phenomena here, like spinning compasses and trees that lean towards the centre of the Mystery Spot? Theories range from alien spaceships to buried asteroids, but nobody really knows. You can visit the spot between 9am and 5pm any day.

From *www.savvytraveler.org*

4

Thousands have visited this natural phenomenon since its discovery in 1940 and many have returned to show their friends the numerous variations of gravity, perspective, compass, velocity, and height that intrigue the visitor to come again. It's unusual, it's amazing, it's wholesome, interesting entertainment. It's crazy – it's perplexing – it's nature's black magic. That's why it is called the Mystery Spot. The Doubting Thomas who heads for the Spot finds himself among the puzzled when he staggers out to regain his sense of balance and perspective.

From *www.mysteryspot.com*

Explaining complicated processes

Even if you understand something, it isn't always easy to explain it to others, because they may not know the terms you use or understand the concepts that lie behind them.

Activity 2: Simplifying

Here a scientist explains how he thinks the Mystery Spot works. Your task is to find the main ideas and explain them in simple everyday terms using five or six sentences.

'All the visual illusions in the Mystery House derive from the fact that the house is tilted,' said William Prinzmetal, adjunct associate professor of psychology.

'You know the house is tilted, but you don't know how much. Everything is tilted. You can't look outside and get a horizon, so you think that what you see is right. It's very compelling,' said Prinzmetal, an expert on perception who has been to the Mystery Spot a dozen times. Although he has studied these illusions, he said his visual perceptions still are distorted when he goes into the house, which is tilted at a 20-degree angle from the ground.

It doesn't take a scientist to know that cockeyed rooms affect perception. If floors are slanted, for instance, people will hang pictures on a slant.

But what has not been known before is that when the perceiver's body also is tilted, the distorting impact on vision is greatly magnified – up to two or three times the effect of slanting the visual field alone.

'In the tilted condition, you are much more affected by the immediate visual context,' said Prinzmetal, who has tested dozens of subjects in a laboratory chair tilted at a 30-degree angle. In that position, he tests their ability to line up vertical dots in a slanted matrix in a darkened room where they have no clue to the true horizon. With their bodies tilted, he said, people's perceptual distortion more than doubles, compared to when they see the same matrix from a level chair.

'We are such visual animals,' said Prinzmetal. 'The mechanism in us that's responsible for determining the horizontal and vertical is mostly affected by what we see. If the context is screwy, that will throw off what we see as vertical and horizontal.'

From *The Berkeleyan, www.berkeley.edu*

Simplified explanations
Advice:

- Look for the main points by underlining or highlighting them.
- Don't go for 'translation'. Give the gist in your own words.
- Use everyday words and don't get too detailed.

A useful order for explaining things:

1 Start by saying what the issue, process or problem is.
2 Summarise the principle on which it works.
3 Say how it is set up or starts.
4 Explain what effect this has.
5 Explain any other consequences.
6 Explain away any problems with your theory.
7 Sum up again in different words.

Describing abstract ideas

Descriptions of people, places and events are easy because people have seen things like them before. Describing ideas and theories is more difficult because they are abstract so there is less to picture.

Activity 3: Explaining

1 An oral task in pairs:

- Explain to a super-smart robot what sorrow is. The robot doesn't have feelings, so it won't understand substitute words like *sadness*.

- Describe how money works for a remote people who do not use money but instead trade food and goods.

2 Afterwards, discuss:

- what was difficult to explain, and why

- what helped, and why.

3 Write up one of the explanations.

Explaining abstract ideas
It helps if you:

- start by saying what the purpose is

- state the principle on which it works

- compare it to something your reader does know: *It's like...*

- follow a similar sequence to the order given above for explanations.

Test it

Imagine you make contact with people who lived 1000 years ago. After spending a day in our time, they are curious to understand a number of things that we take for granted. Explain the following in three or four sentences each:

- the motor car
- electricity
- cinema.

What you get marks for

The purpose of the machine is clear
(0.5 mark for each machine)   1.5 marks

The principle on which it works is made clear
(1 mark each machine)   3 marks

The 'how' is well-explained
(1 mark for each machine)   3 marks

The language is plain and uses everyday words
(0.5 mark for each machine)   1.5 marks

Good use is made of analogy in one of the explanations   1 mark

Total   **10 marks**

Note

You can find more information about the Mystery Spot on the Internet at *www.mysteryspot.com*

14. Persuade, argue, advise

In this masterclass you will learn how to:

- challenge an argument
- defend an argument
- offer balanced advice.

You already know how to present a point of view and to give reasons to support it. In this masterclass you will learn how to respond to an argument you do not agree with.

Challenging an argument

There are many ways to refute an argument:

- by undermining the logic of the argument
- by offering counter-arguments and counter-evidence
- by putting forward a higher 'moral' argument
- by casting doubt on the motives of supporters
- by making people think about the bad consequences of the argument.

Nelson Mandela undermines an argument

The government often answers its critics by saying that Africans of South Africa are economically better off than the inhabitants of the other countries in Africa. Our complaint is not that we are poor by comparision with people in other countries, but that we are poor by comparison with white people in our own country, and that we are prevented by legislation from altering this imbalance.

Nelson Mandela at his trial, 9 October 1963

Activity 1: The rights of burglars

Many people think that the law is wrong, and that criminals caught in the act should not be protected by the law. Think of ways to refute the arguments below, and write up your case in two or three short paragraphs.

The case is true. The argument is:

- The burglar has rights, the same as anyone else.
- It is illegal to injure another person deliberately, so the homeowner committed a crime.
- The reason for the attack is no defence.
- The burglar will suffer for the rest of his life from the scars on his face.

Help ▶▶

Responding to an argument

- Acknowledge the points made: *Of course we all understand the importance of remaining with the law, but...*
- Remain polite.
- Appeal to common sense: *Surely we aren't claiming that burglars have a right to steal undisturbed?*
- Try rhetorical questions: *Do we really believe that families should stand by as burglars steal their possessions?*
- Speak for a wide range of people: *We all have a responsibility to protect our homes and families.*

Activity 2: Defending an argument

Now consider the case from the other side. What arguments can you make in response?

Defending an argument

- Accept the feelings but insist on the logic: *I understand your frustration, but...*

- State the point of principle at stake: *No one is above the law.*

- Take your opponent's view to extremes: *If we make exceptions, who is to say what other groups will rise above the law, making one law for us and another for them?*

- Offer other ways to solve their problem: *The proper way to tackle thieves is not to resort to violence but to...*

- Avoid all this by anticipating their objections and getting in first.

Acknowledging other points of view

Referring to the views expressed by the other side is a good idea because:

- it proves you are listening
- it makes you look polite
- it gives the impression that you can deal with it.

Phrases to use:

- *I understand your feelings of..., but...*
- *No one will wish to disagree with the idea of..., but...*
- *We are agreed on one thing, that is..., but...*
- *I accept your argument that..., but challenge your conclusion that...*

Balanced advice

Every course of action has advantages and disadvantages. When you advise people, you should be open with them about the pros and cons of each option.

A good plan compares the main points of an argument. For example:

	To stay on into sixth form	To leave and get a job
Introduction	Most people choose to stay on	A few people choose to leave (and some train on the job)
Getting qualifications	You need A levels for many jobs and to go to university	Experience may count for more in a job that doesn't need A levels
Earning money	In the long run, qualifications earn more money	You earn money and can afford to do things right away
Changing your mind	Once you leave, you can't easily change your mind	You can go to college if you change your mind about study
Enjoyment	Some people feel trapped and bored by school	Some people feel trapped and bored in their jobs

This plan can be written up by comparing them point by point:

1 The choice facing 16-year-olds.
2 Qualifications.
3 Earning.
4 Changing your mind.
5 Enjoyment.
6 Summarise the benefits and drawbacks of staying on.
7 Summarise the benefits and drawbacks of getting a job instead.
8 Recommendation: who should consider leaving to get a job.

Planning a paragraph

Paragraph 3 can cover both sides of the argument in this way:

- why earnings are worth considering
- earnings if you stay on
- earnings if you leave to work
- conclusion/recommendation.

Earnings are an important because money allows you to be independent. If you stay on at school, you will spend another two years depending on pocket money and part-time jobs. In the long run, however, your qualifications will help you into a better-paid job. If, on the other hand, you leave school, then you will have money in your pocket right away. Your earnings will give you a certain amount of freedom and independence, but later you will find it hard to gain promotion, and over a lifetime your earnings will be lower than those of a person with qualifications. Unless you really dislike school and have a good job to go to, the best advice is to stay on.

Activity 3: Paragraph of advice

Plan, then write one of the other paragraphs.

Activity 4: Balanced advice

1 Draw a grid to compare the arguments for and against the right of parents to smack their children.

2 Plan, then write, a paragraph for one of your points.

3 Write one paragraph summarising either all the points *for* or all the points *against*.

Help ▶▶

Offering advice

- Be honest.
- Cover each point from both sides of the argument.
- Leave the decision to the reader.
- Only go as far as saying which choice would suit particular people in certain situations.
- Be open about disadvantages, even if the arguments in favour are very strong.
- Don't use the first person (*I*) unless you know the reader personally.
- For formal or public writing use *one* or, better still, avoid using a pronoun at all.

Useful words and phrases

One should bear in mind that...

Balanced against this is... However,...

On the other hand,... Alternatively,...

This option would suit...

Before deciding, one should...

Most people choose to...

>> Test it))

Your headteacher is seeking the views of staff, pupils and parents about a plan to introduce a new six-term year, each term being six weeks long, with two weeks' holiday between each term. The arguments for this plan are:

- longer, more restful holidays spread across the year
- shorter terms mean better concentration and less tiredness
- termly topics get the same amount of time
- teachers get regular breaks to plan lessons and mark folders
- family holidays can be taken at cheaper times of year
- the pace of learning is kept up, not lost in the long summer holiday.

Write three short paragraphs refuting this argument.

What you get marks for

Acknowledging the arguments made	1 mark
Clarifying the principle(s) at stake	1 mark
Undermining the arguments presented	1 mark
Offering other ways to solve the problems presented	2 marks
Making your own arguments clear and strong	2 marks
Overall politeness	1 mark
Overall persuasiveness	2 marks
Total	**10 marks**

15. *Analyse, review, comment*

In this masterclass you will learn how to:

- write an analysis
- write a review
- comment fairly.

Analysis

To analyse means to explain or interpret something so that others understand what it is, how it works and why it is significant. We often analyse:

- people's motives
- the significance of historical events
- the deeper meaning of a poem or an expression
- why something has happened
- political developments
- how systems and organisations work.

Analysis often boils down to understanding cause and effect, explaining how things fit and work together. It pays attention to the details. Analysis often follows a pattern:

The writer mentions something that seems true to him.

↓

He describes what he means.

↓

He offers an interpretation or explanation of it.

↓

He gives an example as evidence that illustrates his point.

↓

He explains how the example justifies the point.

↓

He may offer more justification.

↓

He then explains its wider significance.

Activity 1: The analysis sequence

Match the sequence with the sentences in the following analysis:

Pleasers

Pleasers are people who try to gain friendship and attention by striving to please others, even if it means that they lose out. Typically, they buy gifts, lend money, run errands, do favours and give compliments in the hope that this will make them friends. Pleasers learned early on in life that the way to enchant their parents was to be 'good' and 'helpful' and 'kind', but they never learned that this behaviour is not always appropriate outside the family circle. Marta, for example, is viewed with suspicion by her friends because she offers them money and sweets in the playground. They avoid her because this makes them uneasy; they suspect she is trying to buy their friendship instead of earning it. In fact, Marta is using a strategy that worked well at home, and she is confused by their rejection. People who try too hard to please others are really still trying to please their parents.

Activity 2: Write an analysis

Now try your own analysis of one of the following personality types, by using the sequence:

- bullies
- hangers-on
- cynics
- loners
- leaders
- skivers.

Literary analysis

The writing sequence can be used for the literary analysis of poems, novels and plays. You can use the sequence to write a paragraph about a key point.

- The example may be a quotation from the text.
- The explanation will show how effects are created.

Review

A review helps readers to make up their minds whether they would enjoy a particular activity. It offers them a personal view by someone who has already tried it. You can review:

- TV programmes
- computer games
- films
- books
- plays
- restaurants
- holiday resorts
- new cars
- new CDs
- concerts.

Help ▶▶

Writing a review

- Never give away the ending.
- Give enough information to make a decision, but not enough to spoil it.
- You can use *You* to address the reader.
- Use the present tense.
- Talk about the book or film, not about you and your reactions.
- Respect the fact that other people may like different things.
- Make a clear recommendation.
- Go for an equal mix of information and judgement.

Reviews often follow a sequence:

What it is and why it might be of interest.

Summary of content.

What is typical about it, e.g. the style.

What is most successful or likely to please.

What is less successful.

A judgement or recommendation.

Most reviews are short because they appear in newspapers along with others.

Reviewers will try to cover all the points, but save space by condensing two or three of them into one sentence.

Activity 3: The review sequence

How many of the points in the sequence can you find in these reviews:

Film review

Air Force One

Director: Wolfgang Petersen, 1997

Harrison Ford dominates this non-stop action movie as a two-fisted US President taking on a gang of terrorists who hijack the President's 747 on a flight from Moscow to Washington. Petersen handles the claustrophobic setting with the same authority he brought to *Das Boot* but the East European enemies (led by Gary Oldman as an Afghan war veteran) are unduly demonised and the ending is embarrassingly triumphalist.

TV review

99 Things to do before you die

The first programme in a new, 10-part series in which four presenters undertake daring – sometimes to the point of silliness – tasks. One step away from *Jackass*.

From the *Observer*, **13 April 2003**

Activity 4: Write a review

Use the sequence to write two reviews of a book, film or TV programme you have seen, using just two or three sentences each.

Commentary

'Comment' is a word we use about speech, but it can also be used in writing. Written commentary reflects on things as they happen. For example, sports commentary offers views about a game when it is happening. Political commentary offers views about world events as they unfold.

Examples of comment:

- newspaper editorials
- letters in a newspaper
- sports commentary.

Help ▶▶

Features of commentary

- is brief
- tries to make sense of things as they are happening
- makes an educated guess about what it all means
- often uses the present tense and first person
- may speculate about what might happen next.

Activity 5: Features of commentary

What features of commentary can you spot in this editorial?

Every August A level results come out, greeted by the same headlines: 'Passes Reach Record High'. It has been the same story every year without fail since 1982.

While this year's students and their families celebrate, there is inevitably bitterness brought about by the annual improvements, which is reflected in many newspaper stories.

Firstly, there is the concern about the softening up of exams themselves. The conspiracy theory is that the government is able to boost grades artificially to reflect well upon itself.

There remains an understandable feeling of envy among some members of older generations who did not benefit from today's high standards of education and feel relatively underqualified. Perhaps stories of easier exams are popular because of this underlying bitterness.

But the truth is that students today work very hard. And anecdotal evidence suggests that a larger proportion of youngsters are taking qualifications seriously.

Talk of 'dumbing-down' is unfair to the students and their teachers, who have worked very hard to achieve what they have this year.

Editorial from the *Surrey Advertiser*, 15 August 2003 (slightly abridged)

Activity 6: Write a commentary

Write a three-sentence comment for a magazine about the announcement this week that two famous Hollywood couples are to be divorced and marry each other's partners.

▶▶ Test it ⑴

A 56-year-old countess was arrested yesterday for stealing a cashmere jumper from a high street store. She was spotted by store detectives concealing the jumper in a shopping bag. The countess, who is a multi-millionairess, was charged with theft and released on bail.

Write an analysis of why very rich people sometimes steal things.

What you get marks for

For including at least five of the steps in an analysis	up to 5 marks
For providing an interesting interpretation	up to 3 marks
For overall effect	2 marks
Total	**10 marks**

16. Imagine, explore, entertain

In this masterclass you will learn how to:

- imagine, explore and entertain in non-fiction
- get the main points across and bring the facts to life
- exploit the poetry in language even in non-fiction.

Getting the main points across

There are several things you can do to make your main points clear:

- repeat a point in simpler language
- say what it is *not*
- illustrate the point so readers can *see* what you mean
- signal the important points, e.g. *The main point is...*
- go step by step through the points, e.g. *Firstly...*

Activity 1: Fossil

This paragraph is about a fossil found in 1924. It was the skull of a child that lived two million years ago.

- What were the two main points? (Answers at the end of the masterclass.)
- How did the writer bring them out?

Dart instantly recognised two extraordinary features. One is that the foramen magnum (that is, the hole in the skulls that the spinal cord comes up through to the brain) is upright; so that this was a child that held its head up. That is one man-like feature; for in monkeys and apes the head hangs forward from the spine, and does not sit upright on top of it. And the other is the teeth. They are always tell-tale. Here they are small, they are square – these are still the child's milk teeth – they are not the great, fighting canines that the apes have. That means that this was a creature that was going to forage with its hands and not its mouth.

From *The Ascent of Man* **by Jacob Bronowski**

Bringing factual information to life

You can bring facts to life in several ways. Here, Jacob Bronowski explains that animals adapt to live in their environment:

Animals adapt to their environment

Every landscape in the world is full of exact and beautiful adaptations, by which an animal fits into its environment like one cog-wheel into another. The sleeping hedgehog waits for spring to burst its metabolism into life. The humming bird beats the air and dips its needle-fine beak into hanging blossoms. Butterflies mimic leaves and even noxious creatures to deceive their predators. The mole plods through the ground as if he had been designed as a mechanical shuttle.

From *The Ascent of Man* by Jacob Bronowski

The writer uses several methods to make the facts vivid by:

- illustrating his main point
- asking us to picture the examples very precisely, e.g. *needle-fine beak*
- making useful comparisons, e.g. *designed as a mechanical shuttle, like one cog-wheel into another*
- offering thought-provoking claims, e.g. *butterflies mimic leaves.*

He also makes a complex idea quite simple by:

- keeping to well-known examples
- repeating the sentence structure so you know what to expect
- mixing scientific terms with everyday words to keep it more familiar.

Activity 2: Machu Picchu

What devices are used in this extract to bring the facts to life?

Machu Picchu: the remains of an Inca city in South America

The specialists are gone: their work has been destroyed. The men who made Machu Picchu – the goldsmith, the coppersmith, the weaver, the potter – their work had been robbed. The woven fabric has decayed, the bronze has perished, the gold has been stolen. All that remains is the work of the masons, the beautiful craftsmanship of the men who made the city – for the men who make a city are not the Incas but the craftsmen.

From *The Ascent of Man* by Jacob Bronowski

Activity 3: Cave art

Cavemen made wall paintings of animals and hunting. But why? Write a paragraph in which you offer some reasons.

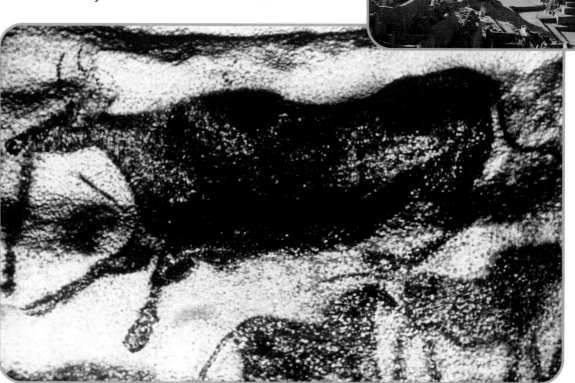

Afterwards, turn to the end of this masterclass to find Jacob Bronowski's attempt at the same task.

Exploiting the poetry in language

When you analyse literature, you study how writers use:

Words

- telling choice of words
- bias in words
- ideas or images associated with words
- repetition of linked or similar words.

Imagery

- use of visual images
- drawing attention to certain details
- appeals to the senses (colour, smell, touch, etc.)
- use of metaphors and similes.

Sound effects

- rhythm and pace
- rhymes
- alliteration
- onomatopoeia.

Expression

- what you notice about the narrator
- the tone
- the degree of formality
- simplicity/complexity.

Sentences

- the structure of sentences
- length and complexity of sentences
- active or passive voice
- type of verbs used.

Structure and organisation

- how it is chunked
- how it is put in order
- the main focuses
- layout – headings, boxes, arrows.

You can do the same for non-fiction.

Activity 4: Cave dwellers

Notice how the writer uses literary effects in this factual writing:

> And yet when we reflect, what is remarkable is not that there are so few monuments, but that there are any at all. Man is a puny, slow, awkward, unarmed animal – he had to invent a pebble, a flint, a knife, a spear. But why to all these scientific inventions, which were essential to his survival, did he add those arts that now astonish us: decorations with animal shapes? Why, above all, did he come to caves like this, live in them, and then make paintings of animals not where he lived but in places that were dark, secret, remote, hidden, inaccessible?

From *The Ascent of Man* **by Jacob Bronowski**

1 Notice how he uses the list of details to illustrate man's inventions: *a pebble, a flint, a knife, a spear*. And notice how each tool is more sophisticated than the one before it in the list.

• Find two other examples of lists.

2 Notice how he chooses words to emphasise man's helplessness: *puny, slow*.

• Find two further words that suggest man's helplessness.

• Find two different words that also suggest how surprisingly gifted cave dwellers were.

3 Notice how we are asked to see both sides of the case by contrasting one phrase against another: *not that there are so few monuments, but that there are any at all*.

• Find two other examples of contrasted phrases.

Activity 5: The first cave paintings

Try using some of the same techniques in a paragraph of your own in which you invite your reader to imagine the first man making his first attempt to paint. You could start: *We can only guess how the first man made the first painting. Maybe…*

Test it))))

Write a paragraph about the value of archaeology. Inspire your reader with the thought that looking into the distant past is worthwhile and important. You could start: *Archaeology is much more than just digging up old bones. When we search for...*

What you get marks for

For bringing out one or two main points clearly	2 marks
For bringing factual information to life with detailed images, thought-provoking ideas and well-explained ideas	3 marks
For using poetic language	3 marks
For overall effect	2 marks
Total	**10 marks**

ANSWERS

Fossil

The ape walked on its hind legs and used its hands. You can tell this because of the position of the spine and the way it used its hands to feed.

Cave art

I think that the power that we see expressed here for the first time is the power of anticipation: the forward-looking imagination. In these paintings the hunter was made familiar with dangers which he knew he had to face but to which he had not yet come. When the hunter was brought here into the secret dark and the light was suddenly flashed on the picture, he saw the bison as he would have to face him, he saw the running deer, he saw the turning boar. And he felt alone with them as he would in the hunt. The moment of fear was made present to him; his spear–arm flexed with an experience which he would have and which he needed not to be afraid of. The painter had frozen a moment of fear, and the hunter entered it through the painting as if through an air-lock.

From *The Ascent of Man* by Jacob Bronowski

17. Leaving spaces for the imagination

In this masterclass you will learn how to:

- help your reader to be more actively involved
- fire your reader's imagination
- inspire your reader.

How readers join in

Reading is a joining-in activity. The mind is active.

Activity 1: Reading

1   As you read this extract, notice what you do with your mind and eyes.
2   Discuss what you saw, thought or did, and compare this with the people around you. How similar were your responses?

'You've got to get a ladder out and climb up and see if everything's all right in Miss Porteus's bathroom,' she said.

'Oh all right,' I said.

So I heaved our ladder over the boards and then ran it up to Miss Porteus's bathroom window. I climbed up. That was the picture they took of me later on: up the ladder, pointing to the bathroom window, which was marked with a cross. All the papers had it in.

What I saw through the bathroom window, even through the frosted glass, was bad enough, but it was only when I had telephoned to the police station and we had forced an entrance that I saw how really terrible it was.

Miss Porteus was lying on the bathroom floor with a bullet wound in her chest. We banged the door against her head as we went in. She had been dead for some time I could almost calculate how long, because of the light. She was in a cerise pink nightgown and the blood had made a little rosette on her chest.

'Bolt the garden gate and say nothing to nobody,' the sergeant said.

I said nothing. The next morning all Claypole knew that Miss Porteus had been murdered, and by afternoon the whole of England knew.

From *Shot Actress – Full Story* by H.E. Bates

Help ▶▶

How readers join in

Readers like to get involved in what they read. They do this by:

- seeing images of the people and events
- remembering similar people and events in their own lives
- wondering and guessing what will happen next
- imagining themselves in the same situation
- feeling involved, e.g. feeling sorry for a character
- asking themselves questions, e.g. *Why is he doing that?*
- going back to check, e.g. for clues, for sense
- updating their impressions, e.g. *Maybe he isn't the murderer*
- rereading the good bits
- reacting, e.g. with surprise or boredom
- hoping for and expecting things, e.g. a happy ending
- making judgements, e.g. *This is boring, Liked the last book better*
- comparing, e.g. *This is just like...*

Inviting the reader to take part

The art of good story writing is to invite the reader to take part. This means that you have to put in hints, mysteries and room for them to 'see' the story in their own way. You can do this in a number of ways:

1. Conjure up an image

Get them to see images by offering a sharp visual detail and let them fill in the full picture. For example:

> She was in a cerise pink nightgown and the blood had made a little rosette on her chest.

From *Shot Actress – Full Story* by H.E. Bates

The woman herself is not described, but the writer has used two striking details to prompt your visual imagination: striking colour and the image of the rosette.

Activity 2: Making an image

Describe a different victim using two details that will prompt your readers to make their own image. Compare efforts, and agree which ones work best and why.

2. Suggest a bigger picture

Sometimes writers cluster several small details to suggest a much bigger picture.

> That afternoon Claypole was besieged by hundreds of people who had never been there before. They moved past Miss Porteus's shop and mine in a great stream, in cars and on foot and pushing bicycles, staring up at the dead actress's window.

From *Shot Actress – Full Story* by H.E. Bates

Details are crammed together to create an impression of a big bustling crowd.

Activity 3: Finding details

1   Find in the extract:
*   three different ways of suggesting a huge number, including two metaphors that convert the huge number into an image
*   three details that suggest a great variety.

2   Describe wedding guests emerging from the ceremony. In two sentences, try to capture the appearance and atmosphere of the group by clustering details.

3. Make a mystery

Hook your reader by creating small mysteries to solve, questions to answer, and by making the reader wait for an answer. For example:

> What I saw through the bathroom window, even through the frosted glass, was bad enough, but it was only when I had telephoned the police station and we had forced an entrance that I saw how really terrible it was.

From *Shot Actress – Full Story* by H.E. Bates

Notice how you are first excited, and then kept waiting.

Activity 4: Mysteries

Find:

* two techniques used by the writer to emphasise how awful it is
* three ways the writer keeps the reader dangling.

Activity 5: Hooking the reader

1   What strategies are used here to hook the reader's curiosity?

> That night, when I went to bed, the light was burning in Miss Porteus's bathroom, but I couldn't see Miss Porteus. Then when I went to the bathroom next morning the light was burning. I said 'Hullo, Miss Porteus left the light on all night', but I thought no more about it. Then when I went up at mid-day the light was still on. It was still on that afternoon and it was on all that night.

From *Shot Actress – Full Story* by H.E. Bates

2   Write a paragraph to hook the reader and keep him or her guessing. The paragraph should tell about one night when you are alone in the house, you answer a knock at the door but no one is there.

4. Get the reader personally involved

To get your readers personally involved, you have to write so that:

- they 'live' the event, even if it's not written as *I*
- the sensations of sight, sound, smell, touch and taste are stimulated
- they are reminded of similar experiences they have had themselves
- mood and feelings are strongly signalled
- they care what happens next.

Activity 6: Living the event

What strategies does the writer use here to get the reader involved?

Deciding to make the dive into an underwater tunnel

In another four days, his mother said casually one morning, they must go home. On the day before they left, he would do it. He would do it if it killed him, he said defiantly to himself. But two days before they were to leave his nose bled so badly that he turned dizzy and had to lie limply over the big rock like a bit of seaweed, watching the thick red blood flow on to the rock and trickle slowly down to the sea. He was frightened. Supposing he turned dizzy in the tunnel? Supposing he died there, trapped? Supposing – his head went round, in the hot sun, and he almost gave up.

In the underwater tunnel

He got his head in, found his shoulders jammed, moved them in sidewise, and was inside as far as his waist. He could see nothing ahead. Something soft and clammy touched his mouth, he saw a dark frond moving against the greyish rock, and panic filled him. He thought of octopuses, of clinging weed.

From *Through the Tunnel* by Doris Lessing

Activity 7: Involving the reader

- Imagine you are small, and your big brother or sister is pushing you on the swing in the park, but teasing you by pushing higher and higher. Write a paragraph in the first person (*I*) in a way that will make the reader feel anxious and sorry for you.

- A teenager is standing on rocks by the sea, ready to jump in. The water is dark. The bottom can't be seen. The teenager hesitates. Write a paragraph in the third person *(he or she)* which makes you feel for them.

Test it

Write three paragraphs:

Paragraph 1 – You are at home alone when you become aware of something not quite right in your home. Hook the reader's curiosity.

Paragraph 2 – You begin to search around to pinpoint what is wrong. Make your reader feel anxious for you.

Paragraph 3 – Find something. Make the reader see it in their mind.

What you get marks for

For two different strategies for hooking the reader's curiosity	3 marks
For two different strategies for making the reader anxious for you	3 marks
For two different strategies for making the reader see it in his or her mind	3 marks
For overall effect	1 mark
Total	**10 marks**

E. IMPROVING YOUR NARRATIVE WRITING

18. Defining your characters

In this masterclass you will learn how to:

- use a defining feature to reveal character
- reveal characters in the way they behave
- use symbolism and suggestion to suggest what they are like.

You can convey character directly:

- describe how they look and what they do
- tell the reader what they are like, e.g. mean, dishonest.

For more depth, you can also reveal characters indirectly:

- the way they behave, talk and think
- a defining feature or symbol that sums up their true character.

Read the following extract:

> Into the leafy, clean-smelling corner went the rabbit hutch, and the pregnant rabbit within it.
>
> 'Poor thing, she doesn't know what's happening to her.'
>
> Martha kneeled on the ground to have a closer look at the rabbit, and her husband leaned over her, propping himself on a corner of the hutch with one hand. His movements were all quick and angular, and he made too many of them; the eye of an onlooker might have been tempted to skip the lightly dressed, light-coloured husband, and rest on the wife. She could comfortably have taken the scrutiny, for she was small and dark and pretty enough, with her broad brow and wide brown eyes. But she too – like her husband – had the strained and guilty air of the perpetually well-intentioned.

From _The Little Pet_ by Dan Jacobson

Activity 1: Revealing personality

What methods does the writer use to reveal the characters? Check your answers at the end of this masterclass.

Using a defining feature

Great writers do not try to tell everything. They pick just one or two things that define the character. Notice how this writer works:

> It was their laugh that betrayed them: only two people who had lived together for some years and were very keen on meeting each other at all points could have laughed so much like each other. It was a practised, accommodating, nervous laugh that they both had, a laugh that never lasted long but was always quick to come again, with a rattle in their throats and a chatter between their teeth. It was a pity that little Francis, their only son, who was standing silently by, did not join in their laughter too.

From *The Little Pet* by Dan Jacobson

You should have picked up that they are close but over-anxious to agree. Their behaviour is not easy or natural. The writer uses their fake laughter as a way of defining their relationship. It is a sort of symbol.

Activity 2: Defining features

1   Think of a defining feature you could use to suggest:
* a couple on the verge of divorce
* a child who is too eager to please
* an older woman who is afraid to let go of her youth
* a highly-strung, over-anxious man.

2   Write a paragraph about one of them.

Revealing character through behaviour

In the extract opposite, the couple bring home a pregnant rabbit.

Activity 3: Revealing character

Read the following extract and discuss how their behaviour reveals their true characters. Afterwards, look for confirmation at the end of the masterclass.

'You'll love playing with her,' Martha said.

'Yes,' the little boy said.

'Oh, see what she's doing now,' Francis senior said. He and Martha were standing arm-in-arm, so he could easily wheel her round to see. The boy stepped forward carefully to see too, and his parents, together, made way for him, grateful for the interest he was showing. The rabbit had been bought for him, after all, and they let him stand in front of them and look. They could see easily enough, over his head.

The rabbit had been bought for little Francis, and how the parents worked in the next few weeks at the fun the rabbit was going to provide him. How assiduously they cleaned out the hutch every day and saw to it that there was fresh water for the rabbit to drink and fresh grass for the rabbit to lie on. When it rained they brought the hutch into the kitchen and kept it there, though it was quite a job for Francis to bring the clumsy contraption of wood and wire netting through the door without scratching the paint on the doorposts, and Martha found it very much in the way when she was cooking. They fed the rabbit lettuce and carrots and cabbage leaves, even though carrots, particularly, were dishearteningly expensive that season. And they watched the rabbit, talked to the rabbit, put their fingers through the wire and waved them at the rabbit, tried to get the rabbit to answer their calls, invented names for the rabbit, discarded these names and invented better ones. They said the rabbit looked like a grandmother, so they called it Granny; they said the rabbit looked like the villain in a Western, so they called it Pardner; sometimes it simply looked sweet, they said, like a bunny that had something to do with an Easter egg or a cold little bunny on a Christmas card, and then they admitted, laughing rapidly and leaning against each other, that they didn't know what they should call it except a darling of a bunny brer rabbit.

From *The Little Pet* by Dan Jacobson

Activity 4: Behaviour

1 Imagine a woman who is sly, jealous and spiteful. Imagine her at a wedding, dinner party or other family event. Also imagine her behaving politely, but underneath simmering with spite against some of the people there.

2 Write two paragraphs in which her behaviour reveals her true character.

Revealing character by symbolism and suggestion

Writers sometimes suggest what characters are like by linking them with an object. Weather, for example, is often used to suggest character. Thunderstorms are linked with evil and danger; sunny spring days are linked with happiness, romance and a fresh start.

Activity 5: Famous character symbols

Can you think of any characters in books, films or TV who are defined by:

- their pets?
- an item of clothing?
- where they live?

Activity 6: Suggestive detail

In the following extract, we get an insight into the way the couple think about the rabbit. Notice what it reveals about the dark side of their personalities.

Martha and Francis could not help thinking that, sometimes, a rabbit was a strange-looking animal. Its face was so strange, with that squared, prominent shape of the central bone, cut sharply downwards, almost hammer-like, like one of those sledge-hammers that men use to break rocks. And then, a long way below the eyes, below the crown of that hammer-like bone, there was the rest of the face: the flat, almost indistinguishable nose, with the rifts of the nostrils concealed unless they were active; and below that secretive nose the mouth, with its upper lip that split so horribly in two when the animal ate, revealing shamelessly pink flesh, gaping like some kind of wound. While above all, mysteriously independent of the rest, the tall ears swung forward or lay back flat or half turned, pivoting in some crafty hollow in the skull. The rabbit was black in colour, but not entirely, for many of the hairs were tipped at the end with a strange rusty colour, a kind of red, the colour of dried blood.

From *The Little Pet* by Dan Jacobson

- Find six details that suggest hidden violence.
- What is it about the rabbit that repels them?
- What is revealed about their states of mind?

> Imagine a child who knows how to please adults and how to tell a convincing lie, but underneath is spiteful and cruel. In three paragraphs, describe how the child persuades an adult to let the child take a pet from its cage, and then secretly torment it.

What you get marks for

Giving the child a defining feature	2 marks
Revealing the child's character in the way he or she behaves	4 marks
Suggesting the child's character using a symbol	2 marks
Overall effect	2 marks
Total	**10 marks**

ANSWERS

Activity 1

The writer describes how they look – she is the dominant one.

- The writer tells the reader at the end what they are like.
- The husband's sharp movements suggest that, beneath his mild appearance, there is some edgy pent-up emotion.

Activity 3

You should have spotted that the parents are trying much too hard to have fun for their son, instead of allowing him to find his own fun. They are overprotective – repressed – even selfish. None of this is said; it is all revealed in the way they behave.

19. *Managing the narrator*

In this masterclass you will learn how to:

- position the reader
- position the narrator
- establish the relationship between the reader and the narrator.

Positioning the reader

Activity 1: Viewpoint

1 Read these extracts on your own and imagine the events in your head:

> The lift had white marble walls, a blue carpet, a silver handrail and no buttons. Roscoe pressed his hand against a small glass panel. A sensor read his fingerprints, verified them and activated the lift. The doors slid shut and the lift rose to the sixtieth floor without stopping. Nobody else ever used it. Nor did it ever stop at any of the other floors in the building.

From *Point Blank* by Anthony Horowitz

> Maria Rosa ran, dodging between beehives, parting two stunted jasmine bushes as she came, lifting her knees in swift leaps, looking over her shoulder and laughing in a quivering, excited way. A heavy jar, swung to her wrist by the handle, knocked against her thighs as she ran. Her toes pushed up sudden spurts of dust, her half-raveled braids showered around her shoulders in long crinkled wisps.

From *María Concepción* by Katherine Anne Porter

- Where were you 'watching' from? Above? Alongside?
- How far away were you? A metre? 10 metres? 100 metres? 1000 metres?
- Compare your answers with other people. Is there general agreement?
- Go back over the extracts and try to find out how the writing positioned you.

It's not just about physical distance (metres, etc.). It's also about emotional distance.

You bring the reader **closer** to the characters by:

- saying or showing how they feel
- showing events from their standpoint
- making the reader live it with them
- emphasising their good qualities
- helping the reader to like and identify with them
- keeping the reader guessing about their fate.

Help ▶▶

Positioning the reader

You can position the reader by:

- including words that suggest the distance, e.g. *far away*, *close by*
- putting things into the picture that make you 'zoom out' or 'zoom in' to catch them
- describing only the things you can see from that distance, e.g. no detail, no close-ups.

You **distance** the reader from your characters by:

- telling what happens instead of 'living' it
- writing in long steady sentences
- writing in calm standard English
- not saying too much about emotions
- not keeping the reader in too much suspense.

Activity 2: Rescue

Write two different paragraphs that describe the rescue of a swimmer in trouble at the local pool.

Paragraph 1 – Position your reader close up to the swimmer in trouble, and very much involved in his or her struggle to survive.

Paragraph 2 – Distance your reader so they understand, but feel detached.

Positioning the narrator

The narrator can approach the reader in different ways. The main ones are:

The detached narrator

- knows about everything, including what characters are thinking
- moves over time and space freely
- doesn't get too involved.

The first person narrator

- speaks as *I*
- has a personality that comes through
- is usually a character in the story.

The attached narrator

- clings close to one of the characters
- shows events as they unfold for that character
- allows us into the thoughts and feelings of that character, but no one else.

The intrusive narrator

- sometimes throws in personal comments about the story or talks directly to the reader, wanting attention
- sometimes plays tricks with the story, e.g. time slips, shifting from character to character, holding back vital information
- sometimes has a personality even though not a character in the story.

The differences aren't hard and fast.

Activity 3: Different types of narrator

1   What type of narrator is featured in each of these extracts?

> I expected every wave would have swallowed us up, and that every time the ship fell down, as I thought, in the trough or hollow of the sea, we should never rise more; and in this agony of mind I made many vows and resolutions, that if it would please God here to spare my life this one voyage, if ever I got once my foot upon dry land again, I would go directly home to my father, and never set it into a ship again while I lived.

From *Robinson Crusoe* by Daniel Defoe

> 'He must propose tomorrow,' thought Rebecca. 'He called me his soul's darling, four times; he squeezed my hand in Amelia's presence. He must propose tomorrow.' And so thought Amelia too. And I daresay she thought of the dress she was to wear as bridesmaid, and of the presents.

From *Vanity Fair* by William Thackeray

> Juan awakened slowly, with long yawns and grumblings, alternated with short relapses into sleep full of visions and clamours. A blur of orange light seared his eyeballs when he tried to unseal his lids. There came from somewhere a low voice weeping without tears, saying meaningless phrases over and over.

From *María Concepción* by Katherine Anne Porter

> About ten o'clock of a dark September evening the Zemstvo doctor Kirilov's only son, six-year-old Andrey, died of diphtheria. As the doctor's wife dropped on to her knees before the dead child's cot and the first paroxysm of despair took hold of her, the bell rang sharply in the hall.

From *Enemies* by Anton Chekov

Afterwards, check your answers at the end of this masterclass.

Activity 4: Quarrel

A quarrel between a man and woman comes to a dramatic conclusion when one of them smashes a plate, shocking the other and thus bringing the quarrel to an end.

Write three sentences about this quarrel, first as a detached narrator, then as a first person narrator, then as an intrusive narrator, and finally as an attached narrator. Compare the effect.

The influence of the narrator

The narrator influences the reader's response by:

- showing only what he or she wants to show
- by passing comments
- by using words that influence feelings.

Here a boy looks in through the window of a pub to see men gambling.

> I sat alone on the shaft of the cart in the narrow passage, staring through a side window of 'The Hare's Foot'. A stained blind was half drawn over it. I could see into half of a smoky, secret, room, where four men were playing cards. One man was huge and swarthy, with a handlebar moustache and a love-curl on his forehead; seated by his side was a thin, bald, pale old man with his cheeks in his mouth; the faces of the other two were in shadow. They all drank out of brown pint tankards and never spoke, laying the cards down with a smack, scraping at their matchboxes, puffing at their pipes, swallowing unhappily, ringing the brass bell, ordering more, by a sign of the fingers, from a sour woman with a flowered blouse and a man's cap.

From *The Peaches* **by Dylan Thomas**

Activity 5: Giving an impression

1   The writer wants to give us a bad opinion of the men.
- Find four details about the setting that make it seem dismal.
- Find five negative words used to describe the men.
- Find three details that suggest that it is probably an illegal meeting.

2   Write three sentences about another man who enters the room, giving the impression that he is the organiser, and is feared by the others.

►► Test it)))

A new pupil is standing at the school gate ready for the first day at school after a move of house.

1 Write the first paragraph of a story about the first day told by a bossy, godlike narrator who takes the story in hand and talks directly to the reader. You could start: *Come with me now to the school gate where we shall find our hero. He doesn't look like much of a hero now, but...*

2 Now try it a different way. Be detached. Leave the reader to work out as much as possible. Offer only facts and observations, do not get involved, and leave out your own opinions and comments. You could start: *Eight-fifty on a cool day in late autumn, and the leaves are falling by the school gate. The school hushes as pupils disappear into lessons. By the gate stands...*

What you get marks for

Paragraph 1

For keeping up the forceful voice of the narrator	1 mark
For talking directly to the reader	1 mark
For keeping up an informal style	1 mark
For making the personality of the narrator interesting or amusing	1 mark
For overall effect	1 mark

Paragraph 2

For sticking to facts and observation	1 mark
For avoiding feelings and opinions	1 mark
For keeping up a formal style	1 mark
For keeping the narrator 'hidden'	1 mark
For overall effect	1 mark
Total	**10 marks**

ANSWERS

Activity 3

The first extract is first person.   The second extract is intrusive.

The third extract is attached.   The fourth extract is detached.

20. Knowing where you are going

In this masterclass you will learn how to:

- work out the main point or moral of your story
- write with your ending in mind
- keep the reader on board to the end.

We often think of endings as the last scene, but a good writer works towards it by:

- making the reader work out how it might end
- making the reader long for a particular ending
- dropping clues about how it might end
- teasing the reader by putting obstacles in the way of the desired ending
- keeping the reader guessing.

Resolutions

The resolution of the story is the way the problems are resolved.

Most stories follow a familiar pattern:

1. We are introduced	2. A problem or conflict arises	3. Things go wrong	4. Things get complicated	5. Things come to a head	6. A solution or part-solution is found	7. Everyone adjusts

The resolution is covered by 6 and 7, but the writer can often be seen preparing for it much earlier. Readers have an urge to see matters resolved, so they are looking for a solution. In a detective story, they look for clues that will identify the villain and bring him or her to justice. In a love story, they are looking for a way to overcome the obstacles that stand between the lovers.

Example

In the story 'Possessions', a penniless mother has to sell one of her two valuable possessions: a piano and a pony. She chooses to sell the pony so that her son can study music. But soon she sees that the pony is being maltreated by its new owner and so she steals it back when it is left standing in the rain outside the pub.

Dando Hamer came up early next morning and Ma was ready for him. Gomer and I were there to see the fun. Dando was very mild and sheepish.

'Morning, Mrs Pritchard,' he said. 'Thank you for putting up the pony.' Ma looked at him without speaking, and he twirled the peak of his cap uneasily. 'It was all a perfect accident,' he went on quite animatedly. 'I was detained, you see, longer than I expected.'

'Dando Hamer,' Ma said with all the scorn she could command, 'you're not fit to brush out the pony's stall!'

Dando bent his head and acknowledges his failings. 'Can I have him now?' he asked after a few long seconds.

Ma quietly folded her apron: 'No, you cannot. The pony is staying with me,' she said.

Dando stiffened and worked himself into a fury. A flood of words poured out, all in a beery jumble. The word *police* was mixed up with them.

From *Possessions* by George Ewart Evans

Activity 1: Looking ahead to the ending

- What would need to happen to make this a happy ending?
- Find hints about the possible ending.
- Do you get a sense that this will be a happy or a tragic ending? Any clues?

Now read on:

'Police!' my mother said quietly. 'Don't you use that word Dando. Just you be thinking what you'll say when I've fetched the Cruelty Inspector to see the pony!'

Dando worked his lips in silence. 'But how can I go on my round?' he whined.

'Davy Prothero Bonanza Stores has just bought a motorcar, and his horse is spare. Go up and ask him to lend you the horse, and take your old cart away from here. I'll pay you back the money you gave me for the pony.'

Dando looked narrowly at my mother. He knew that there were no long stockings hidden in our house. 'When, Mrs Pritchard?' he asked with a polite leer.

'As soon as I've sold the piano. Be off with you now! I can't waste time talking to no purpose.'

From *Possessions* **by George Ewart Evans**

Activity 2: Revising your opinion

- What elements of the ending have fallen into place, and what still needs to be resolved?
- Can you see a way of resolving the story?
- Does it now seem likely to be a happy or tragic ending?

Now read on:

But Dando had suddenly brightened up. The word piano had struck a hidden chord somewhere deep inside him. 'Is that the piano with the green front?' he asked eagerly. 'Wanting to sell it are you?'

'Yes!'

'Can I have a look at it?'

From *Possessions* **by George Ewart Evans**

Activity 3: Further clues

What clues can you find in the extract that set you thinking about a possible ending?

This is going to be a happy ending. The writer soon tells us that the son didn't much like the piano lessons, anyway.

Activity 4: A tragic ending

1   Imagine a tragic ending to the story. What would be in it?

2   Rewrite the conversation so that it leads the reader to a more gloomy conclusion. Prompt the reader to expect the worst.

Endings

Stories end in lots of different ways:

- happy endings
- bitter-sweet endings
- tragic endings
- sting-in-the-tail surprise endings
- cliffhanger endings
- question mark endings
- cheating (*Then I woke up and it was all a dream...*).

Activity 5: Famous examples

1   Can you think of well-known examples of these different endings?

2   What often happens in a typical happy ending? Spend three minutes discussing this.

3   Afterwards, turn to the answers at the end of the masterclass.

The moral of the story

The moral of the story is its main lesson or message. For example:

- Crime doesn't pay.
- Love is more important than money.
- Treat others as you would have them treat you.

Activity 6: Morals

Think of the endings of well-known stories from books, TV or films.
Can you work out their morals?

Activity 7: Alternative endings

Your plot: An old lady is cheated by an antique dealer who gives her £500 for an item that he knows to be worth £50,000.

1 Discuss how you could develop the story in three different ways to suit these endings:

- a sting-in-the-tail ending that proves that things are not always what they seem
- a happy ending that shows that it's never too late to do the right thing
- a bitter-sweet ending that proves that trade is clever, but age is wise.

2 Here is the paragraph which describes the dealer after the old lady has left the shop.

**After she left, the dealer, whose name was _____,
sucked in the air sharply. He ran a hand over the side of the
_____ and whistled out. He hardly dared to breathe.**

Fill in the name of the dealer and the name of the object, and then complete the paragraph in three different ways to fit the endings above.

Test it

Write three paragraphs resolving a story with the following plot:

You receive a small battered parcel posted ten years ago in a faraway place. It contains several mysterious objects but no letter. What can it mean? You research the objects and discover something rather unsettling about them, piecing together a story that links you to the objects. You contact someone who you think might be able to help you, but they tell you to forget it and ask you not to call again.

1 Consider how you might end the story. Write down the way you will resolve the mystery and what the moral will be.

2 Write four or five paragraphs resolving the story.

What you get marks for

Clues about the ending are left	2 marks
The sense of mystery is maintained	2 marks
The reader is kept guessing about the ending	2 marks
The ending fits the moral	1 mark
The ending's not too contrived	1 mark
The overall effect is good	2 marks
Total	**10 marks**

ANSWERS

Activity 5

Features of a typical happy ending

- Justice is done.
- The good characters are rewarded.
- The bad characters are punished.
- The hero gets the girl; the heroine finds love.
- Things are restored to normal.
- Mysteries are explained.
- Only minor characters die – the rest are saved.
- Loose ends are tied up.

F. NOTES

21. Notes to the pupil

1. Have a plan you can hold in your head

Example 1: A piece of personal writing

| Introduction | → | The first time we met | → | How we became friends | → | How we argued | → | Memorable moments | → | Meeting years later | → | What I think now |

Example 2: A history essay

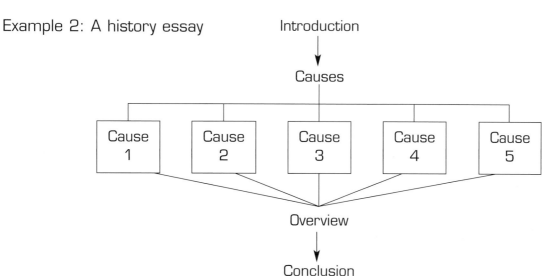

Introduction

↓

Causes

| Cause 1 | Cause 2 | Cause 3 | Cause 4 | Cause 5 |

Overview

↓

Conclusion

2. Stuck for ideas?
Use a planning shape to get ideas flowing

For and against columns

For	Against

Star chart

idea — detail

idea — detail

TOPIC — idea — detail

idea

idea — detail

Never comes out right?
Rehearse the sentences in your head.
If the sentence is too long to remember, at least know how it will end.
Consider breaking it up into two sentences.

3. Sounds flat? Vary the way you start your sentences

Try starting with an adverb:

> <u>Slowly</u> he begins to think there is something wrong.

Or an adjective:

> <u>Talented,beautiful</u> Emma realises she is out of luck at last.

Or with a verb:

> <u>Returning</u> home, she has a sense that every good thing in her life is over.

Or a preposition:

> <u>Beyond</u> the gate, something has stirred in the darkness.

4. Replace some dull verbs with powerful verbs

Example:

>   slithers   gliding
> The creature ~~draws~~ closer to the house, ~~moving~~ on a trail of sticky slime.

5. Replace some general nouns with strong specific nouns

Example:

>   porch   slick
> The creature slithers closer to the ~~house~~, gliding on a ~~trail~~ of
>   mucus
> sticky ~~slime~~.

6. Looks untidy? Line up and leave space

Even the worst handwriting looks better if you stick to the margin and leave space round each answer.

Before:

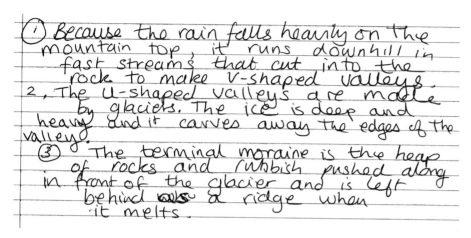

> ① Because the rain falls heavily on the mountain top, it runs downhill in fast streams that cut into the rock to make V-shaped valleys.
> 2, The U-shaped valleys are made by glaciers. The ice is deep and heavy and it carves away the edges of the valley.
> ③ The terminal moraine is the heap of rocks and rubbish pushed along in front of the glacier and is left behind as a ridge when it melts.

After:

> 1. Because the rain falls heavily on the mountain, it runs downhill in fast streams that cut into the rock to make V-shaped valleys.
>
> 2. The U-shaped valleys are made by glaciers. The ice is deep and heavy, and carves away the edges of the valley.
>
> 3. The terminal moraine is the heap of rocks and rubbish pushed along at the front of the glacier and is left behind as a ridge when it melts.

7. Horrible handwriting? Tidy up with six simple rules

1   Slope it all in the same direction (pencil in lines if you have to).

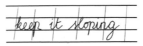

2   Make all the tails the same.

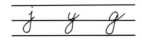

3   Keep it on the line.

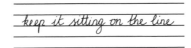

4   Change to a fountain pen with a thick nib.

5   Keep the small letters all the same height.

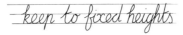

6   Change your worst letters one at a time for a week at
a time.

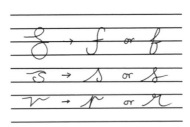

Try sticking to rule 1 for the first week.

Try sticking to rules 1 and 2 for the second week.

Try sticking to rules 1, 2 and 3 for the third week.

And so on...

8. Spelling's a nightmare? Learn the top 5 rules, 50 common words and top tips for learning

1 Plurals

Most plurals just add S.

Some words add ES because they end in a hissing, shushing or buzzing sound. The ES creates an extra syllable.

marsh – marshes   fizz – fizzes

2 Doubling

Why one T in *writing* but two in *written*?

Why one N in *dining* but two in *dinner*?

Here's the trick: listen to the vowel just before it.

- If it's a long vowel (one that says its own name), use a single letter.
- If it's a short vowel, use double letters.

3 Adding prefixes

Just add prefixes. They never change the word.

dis + appear = disappear   dis + satisfied = dissatisfied

4 Adding suffixes

Most suffixes can just be added, but watch out for:

Words ending in consonant + Y, e.g. *pity*

- Change Y to I if you add a suffix, e.g. pitiful, pitied, pitiless.
- But avoid two vowels together, e.g. pitying, not pitiing.

Words ending in consonant + E

- Keep the E in most cases.
- But avoid two vowels together, e.g. boring, not boreing.

5 Take care when two vowels sit together

IE – most common, e.g. thief.

EI – after C, e.g. receive or when it sounds like A, e.g. vein.

A–E – the most common long A spelling, e.g. stale.

O–E – the most common long O spelling, e.g. note.

OW – usually at the end of words, e.g. cow.

OU – usually at the start or in the middle of words e.g. out, mouse.

Fifty words that are often misspelt

Learn them.

1. alcohol	18. health	35. research
2. although	19. height	36. Saturday
3. autumn	20. imaginary	37. secondary
4. beautiful	21. interest	38. separate
5. because	22. knowledge	39. sincerely
6. beginning	23. listening	40. soldier
7. believe	24. marriage	41. stomach
8. business	25. material	42. straight
9. chocolate	26. necessary	43. strength
10. daughter	27. parallel	44. success
11. definitely	28. people	45. surprise
12. design	29. permanent	46. technology
13. environment	30. physical	47. tomorrow
14. February	31. possession	48. Wednesday
15. forty	32. process	49. weight
16. guard	33. receive	50. women
17. happened	34. remember	

Ten ways to remember spellings

- Break it into sounds (a-l-c-o-h-o-l).
- Break it into syllables (re-mem-ber).
- Break it into sections (re + search).
- Use a memory trick (necessary – one collar, two sleeves).
- Think of a word in the same family (e.g. strong – strength).
- Say it as it sounds (Wed-nes-day).
- Words within words (heal in health).
- Refer to etymology (Saturday = Saturn Day).
- Link to word families and learn a key word (height, weight, freight, eight).
- Learning it by looking.

Soundalikes

These words are often mixed up. Here's a way to remember which is which:

Confusions	How to remember which is which
affect/effect	<ul><li>*Affect* is what you do (verb)</li><li>*Effect* is the result (noun)</li><li>If you forget, use *effect* – it's used more often</li></ul>
allowed/aloud	<ul><li>*Allowed* ends in ED because it's a past tense verb: *allow/allowed*</li><li>The word *loud* within *aloud* is a clue</li></ul>
bought/brought	<ul><li>Say it slowly to hear the R</li><li>Link *brought* to *bring*</li></ul>
choose/chose	<ul><li>OO says OO</li><li>Remember the double letter by remembering *Choose cheese*</li></ul>
cloth/clothe	<ul><li>The E at the end makes the O long; compare *not/note*</li></ul>
our/are	<ul><li>*Our* can be linked to the other pronoun *your*</li></ul>
practice/practise	<ul><li>C is the noun</li><li>S is the verb</li><li>Easy-to-hear comparisons: *advice/advise* and *device/devise*</li></ul>
quiet/quite	<ul><li>Say it slowly to hear the E before the T – it makes an extra syllable</li></ul>
threw/through	Learn:<ul><li>I *knew* who *threw* it</li><li>*Through* the *rough* field</li></ul>
their/there	<ul><li>Learn *their heirlooms* as a way of remembering which one means 'belonging to them'</li><li>Link *there* to *here* and *where*</li></ul>
to/too/two	<ul><li>*To* is the most common one if you are not sure</li><li>The double O in *too* reminds you it means *too* many</li><li>*Two* links to *twice*</li></ul>

These are separate words:

- a lot of
- thank you

F. NOTES

22. Notes to parents and helpers

This note contains advice about how to help a young person to compose a piece of writing, and then offers ideas for encouraging better writing.

Helping growing writers

Do you remember when they were very little, and you read a bedtime story? Or when they went to primary school how they brought home books and you listened to them read? The problem with writing is that no one ever writes a story at bedtime or listens to their children writing. It's not obvious how to share writing.

It's the same at school. There's plenty of help to get going, and there's marking afterwards, but something is missing in the middle – help at the time of writing.

This is how to do it.

Getting started

Sit with them before they start and get them to tell you what they have to do. Don't cross-question them: it makes them clam up.

Make sure they know these things before they start:
- the title or question
- the point of doing it
- how long it should be
- what style it should be.

And if you're lucky:
- what the teacher said about the task (if it is a school task)
- the mark scheme (sometimes pasted in the exercise book)
- if they're allowed to word process it.

Ask them to tell you the main things they need to say and what order to say them. This will be the writing plan. You write it. This is going to be harder than you think; it's surprising how often older children start writing without having a map of the writing in their heads. Ask clarifying questions as you go and finish by repeating back the order of points as you understand them.

If you or they find this really difficult, you may need to drop back to an earlier stage of gathering ideas.

Ask them how they're going to start. Some people find this incredibly challenging and they freeze up. If so, leave a space and you can go back to it later. Instead, start with the first proper point.

The process of writing

Ask them to tell you in their own words how they will express the first point or paragraph. If they seem pretty confident about it, get them to write it down and watch what they do.

Hold back on the criticism. It is really tempting to jump in at the first spelling error or offbeat expression and put it right. But don't do it. They will hate it and never want to write with you again. Also, don't do all the work for them even if it makes you feel good, because the idea is to help them to do it for themselves. On the other hand, approve of anything good such as:

- a well-chosen word
- a well-expressed idea
- a good opening line
- spelling a tricky word
- use of links, e.g. conversely, thus, although
- mature expression.

At the end of each paragraph, sum up what is good about the paragraph and allow yourself one other comment. Don't express it as a negative, and avoid interrogation. Make plain and obvious points and speak on your own behalf as a reader. For example:

- I think you've left a letter out of this word.
- I'm not clear what you're saying at the end here.
- So this is everything you want to say on this topic?
- This expression sounds odd to me.
- Check the punctuation in the middle there.
- I think you've missed a comma.

The idea is to alert them to the problem but let them sort it out. Don't abandon them, though. Allow a few moments for them to act. If they're plainly stuck, ask them to tell you what they're thinking.

- Tell me what you're thinking.
- What will you do?
- Tell me how you'll change it.
- Any ideas?

Now you can help by refining their ideas rather than substituting your own. Do this quickly. No slogging.

Getting on with it

Now let them get on with the writing for a while. It's too much to write the whole thing with them. Ask them to call you over when they get to a tricky bit.

The kitchen table is a pretty good place for writing because they can sit at it to write whilst you potter in the background. Stay around, avoid chatting and don't hover. And especially don't go sniping for errors.

When they're done, ask them to read the whole thing to you. This is for them more than it is for you. They will sense the effect of what they've written. Don't interrupt. Make at least two positive comments. Be specific – 'That's okay' won't do; you have to say what is okay, for example: 'The opening is strong, and you make a good point about newspapers.'

Depending on their mood, ask if they want you to proofread it for them or pick up on one point that was unclear during the reading.

Checking

If you proofread, indicate where the problems lie but don't correct it for them. Instead, give them a prompt:

- I think you've got a letter too many in that word – do you know which one it is?
- You've mixed up *there* and *their* – how do you know which is which?
- There's a full stop missing on this line – where should it go?
- There's a punctuation error on this line – can you see it?

Your main aim here is to teach them the right way to do it. But if they are struggling, don't slog. Tell them the general rule and how to correct the mistake. Let them correct it. Ideally, make a note that they can keep as an aide-mémoire. A sheet in a ring binder is good, or a sheet blu-tacked to the kitchen wall.

Showing an interest

You may find over the next day or so that the topic about which you were writing comes into your mind, or something will come up that reminds you of it. Mention it to your offspring: it's good that they know you found it interesting, that you looked beyond the spelling and punctuation. It says that writing has meaning.

Other things you can do to help

1. Help with written homework (but don't do it for them)

Make only constructive comments and ask questions such as these:

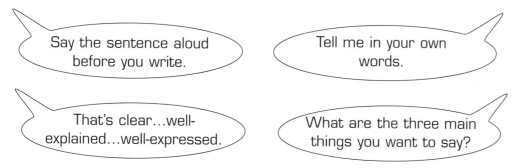

> Say the sentence aloud before you write.

> Tell me in your own words.

> That's clear...well-explained...well-expressed.

> What are the three main things you want to say?

2. Give gifts that encourage writing

e.g. diary, stationery, fountain pen, stamps, card-making software.

3. Play games that improve spelling

e.g. Scrabble, Boggle, Lexicon, crosswords, word searches.

4. Buy an easy-to-read dictionary and a thesaurus

Look for clear print, boldfaced words and simple explanations.

5. Put up spelling checklists

Put them in places where they will be seen often e.g. bedside, toilet door.

6. Ask them to do writing for the family

e.g. shopping lists, packing lists, postcards, emails.

7. Encourage them to read more

Take them to visit libraries and bookshops. Read their set texts. Point out interesting articles. Subscribe to a magazine. Buy book tokens.

8. If they use a word processor, advise them how to use the facilities for checking, editing and presentation

The **checking** facilities include – the spellchecker, thesaurus, grammar check, word count and the track changes facilities. Most software has a setting that underlines spelling errors and grammatical issues as you type.

The **editing** facilities include cut, copy and paste.

The **presentation** facilities are usually listed under a drop-down format menu. It includes font size and shape, borders, shading, bullet styles, paragraph styles, etc. Many programmes now offer help with common layouts such as letters.

Some things that don't work

Forcing them to write

It's not really about writing more; it's about knowing how to compose. Practice is important at a certain stage, but you can end up recycling mistakes. If you want to write with your son or daughter, keep it to a few sentences and focus on expression.

Telling them what to write

If you tell them what to write, you'll get good at it but they will become dependent on you. The main thing is to help them do it for themselves. Ask helpful questions or make broad suggestions.

Expecting perfection

Stick to one or two points of help, and do it little and often. It's demoralising for them if you always expect perfection. Luckily, you have your children for life, so you can afford to take your time.

23. Notes to the teacher
Characteristics of writers at Level 4

The writers at whom this book is targeted are likely to be at Level 4 in writing, even if their reading is in advance of this. Already they will be competent writers with some rhetorical skills. Certainly, most sentences will be accurately punctuated though not necessarily ambitious.

In terms of the National Curriculum, Level 4 writers are described thus:

> **Pupils' writing in a range of forms is lively and thoughtful. Ideas are often sustained and developed in interesting ways and organised appropriately for the purpose of the reader. Vocabulary choices are often adventurous and words are used for effect. Pupils are beginning to use grammatically complex sentences, extending meaning. Spelling, including that of polysyllabic words that conform to regular patterns, is generally accurate. Full stops, capital letters and question marks are used correctly, and pupils are beginning to use punctuation within the sentence. Handwriting style is fluent, joined and legible.**

But this is a 'best fit' descriptor: there will be many writers at Level 4 who turn a good plain sentence and make good plain meanings, but while they can read between the lines when they study fiction, they do not yet 'write between the lines'. Others who are flamboyant writers will not yet have control of the complex sentence, and their punctuation will be wayward when they strive to write elaborate sentences.

Typical of Level 5 writing is a tendency to splash commas around and to be badly in need of semicolons, colons and short sentences when they are needed. On the whole, there is a lot of promise in flamboyant writers of this sort: they are flirting and experimenting with the extended sentence, and the task in this case is to teach them how to control it with punctuation.

More problematic are those pupils who are afraid to make mistakes and so play safe, clinging on to simplistic sentence structures that they can already handle, sticking to words they already spell and rehearsing again text types they have already mastered. These are pupils who work but progress slowly.

We might say of them that their hard work is repaid by a pass mark but no honours. We will meet them later at GCSE unable to get beyond C, or even at A level putting in long hours but hitting a ceiling below the grades that would get them into university. Their conservativism and fear of failure holds them back. Their expression stops developing as an early teenager and, as time goes by, they sound more and more out of their depth, unable to write sentences that can express more complex insights. This is the reason why Level 5 at age 14 is such a good predictor of five good GCSE grades at age 16. Quite simply, you need to be articulate in writing to do well.

Moving from Level 4 to Level 5

Level 5 writers come across as much more organised and controlling, though the level descriptor is rather unhelpful in its fascination with clarity, accuracy and formality.

> **Pupils' writing is varied and interesting, conveying meaning clearly in a range of forms for different readers, using a more formal style where appropriate. Vocabulary choices are imaginative and words are used precisely. Simple and complex sentences are organised into paragraphs. Words with complex regular patterns are usually spelt correctly. A range of punctuation, including commas, apostrophes and inverted commas, is usually used accurately. Handwriting is joined clear and fluent and, where appropriate, is adapted to a range of tasks.**

At Level 5, pupils move beyond 'expressing themselves' to being more manipulative and truly creative: they make conscious choices and have a new passion for order. There is something of the control freak in a Level 5 writer.

The thing that will strike the teacher reading Level 5 work is a new maturity of expression, a literariness in the language. It is the magical effect of the complex sentence. The pupil who has taken command on the complex sentence has entered a new phase of language development that will propel them all the way to adulthood in writing.

The sentence is the single most important thing to teach about writing for pupils at this level. When you can manage the complex sentence, you can 'mean' what you want, you can 'mean' new things. 'Mean' becomes something you do, an active verb.

Using this book

This book is arranged in masterclasses which will fill two or maybe three lessons depending on the length of your lessons. The masterclasses break down quite easily so they can be spread in shorter blocks of around 20 minutes.

They can be used flexibly, for example:

* mini-units positioned between longer units of work
* group study units for up to six pupils at Level 4
* guided writing groups
* a substantial unit of work on *Improving expression.*

All the masterclasses are about the art of expression. Most of them are about sentences and a few are about paragraphs. Text level work is important, of course, but this book focuses on sentences because they have proved more difficult to teach in large classes.

The traditional way of teaching sentences at this level has been in the marking, but that comes too late. The important time is during composition itself, so this book attempts to address that shaping moment. The book is tightly structured to guide pupils through the process, leaving you free to work at close quarters with one or more pupils. They should be used like masterclasses for intensive and high-velocity induction to the art of sentence control.

To add value demonstrate on the board how you would tackle them, composing on the spot and thinking aloud about what you are doing. The purpose of this is to give pupils an insight into the dynamics of composition.

Because you are expecting pupils to improve and revise their expression, they should be doing a lot of amendments. A word processor is an ideal tool, or failing this, a wipe-clean board for drafting.

Acknowledgements

The author and publisher would like to thank the following for:

Copyright text:

pp2, 3 and 4 *Flood* © Richard Doyle, 2002, Arrow. Reprinted by permission of The Random House Group Ltd; pp7, 8 and 12 *The Green Consumer Guide* © John Elkington and Julia Hailes, 1988, Victor Gollancz; pp14 and 16 *The Fabulous Girl's Guide to Decorum* © Kim Izo and Ceri Marsh, 2002, Corgi; p15 'Everyone knows Italians love children. In theory…' © Amanda Craig in the *Observer*, 25 May 2003; pp16 and 17 'Red or dead' © Robin McKie in the *Observer*, 25 May 2003; p17 'Top of the mourning' © Sean O'Hagan in the *Observer*, 18 May 2003; p21 'Magician's London debut in glass coffin' © Adam Smith in *The Times*, 20 August 2003; pp39–40 Guildford Museum, Boat House and History text from *Guildford Short Breaks* © Guildford Borough Council; p41 *Hidden Depths* © Roger Hunt, 2002, Surrey Archaeological Society; pp52, 53 and 54 *Under the Skin* © Michel Faber, 2000, Canongate Books; pp56, 57, 58 and 59 *Spies* © Michael Frayn, 2002, Faber & Faber; pp63, 67 and 68 *Out of the Ancient World* © Victor Skipp, 1967, Penguin; p64 *Red Shift* © Alan Garner, 1973, Collins; p69 *The Oxford Children's Encyclopaedia* © OUP, 1991; pp76 and 77 © Minnesota Public Radio, 2000. All Rights Reserved. www.savvytraveler.org; pp76 and 77 © www.mysteryspot.com; p78 © *The Berkeleyan*, the faculty/staff newspaper of the University of California, Berkeley, 1998, The Regents of the University of California, www.berkeley.edu; p90 © the *Observer*, 13 April 2003; p91 © the *Surrey Advertiser*, 15 August 2003; pp93, 94, 95, 97 and 98 *The Ascent of Man* © Jacob Bronowski, 1973, BBC Books; pp99, 100, 101 and 102 'Shot Actress – Full Story' © H.E. Bates, from *Twenty Tales*, Jonathan Cape and Pollinger Limited; p103 *Through the Tunnel* © Doris Lessing, 1990, Creative Education; pp105, 106, 107 and 109 'The Little Pet' © Dan Jacobson, from *Short Stories of Our Time*, 1963, Chambers Harrap Publishers; p111 *Point Blank* © Anthony Horowitz, 2002, Philomel Books; pp111 and 114 'María Concepción' © Katherine Anne Porter, 1922, from *Flowering Judas*, 1930, Harcourt Brace and Company; p114 *Robinson Crusoe* by Daniel Defoe, 1878; p114 *Vanity Fair* by William Thackeray, 1847; p114 'Enemies' by Anton Chekov, 1887, from *Doctor's Visit*; p115 'The Peaches' © Dylan Thomas, 1940, from *Collected Stories*, Orion; pp118 and 119 'Possessions' © George Ewart Evans, from *Short Stories of Our Time*, 1963, Chambers Harrap Publishers.

Copyright photos and images:

p2 *Thundering Waves* © Guy Motil, CORBIS; p3 *Thames Flood Barrier* © Mykel Nicolaou, REX FEATURES; p5 *Coast Guard Vessel in Stormy Seas* © James A. Sugar, CORBIS; p8 *Herding Cattle Through Corral* © James A. Sugar, CORBIS; p9 'What we throw away every year' from *The Green Consumer Guide* © John Elkington and Julia Hailes, 1988, Victor Gollancz; p10 *A Pile of Junk Mail* © Catherine Gehm, REX FEATURES; p11 *Refuse Tip and Incineration Plant at Marsh Barton* © Nicholas Bailey, REX FEATURES; p12 *Hose* © Sue Hackman; p13 *Bags*, Photodisk; p15 *Family Dinner* © Ariel Skelley, CORBIS; p16 *Mars* © Stocktrek, CORBIS; p19 *Mosquito* © LHT, REX FEATURES; p21 *David Blaine* © HXA, REX FEATURES; p27 *Children at a Birthday Party* © Richard Hutchings, CORBIS; p29 *Fish*, Corel; p30 *Boy in a DT Lesson* © John Walmsley; p32 *Girl Writing* © John Walmsley; p33 *Starting a Race* © David Stoecklein, CORBIS; p36 *Snowboarder Performing Jump* © David Stoecklein, CORBIS; p39 *Guildford Leaflets* © Sue Hackman; p39 *Guildford Museum* and *Guildford Boat House* from *Guildford Short Breaks* © Guildford Borough Council; p40 *Guildford Castle* © Sue Hackman; p42 *Guildford Boat House* leaflet © Guildford Boat House Limited; p42 *Dapdune Wharf* and *River Wey* leaflets © The National Trust; p47 *All you can eat* © Tiger Lil's; p52 *Snow-covered Cumbrian Mountainside Near Windermere, UK* © Michael Busselle, CORBIS; p56 *Suburban Semi in 1930s' Britain* © Hulton-Deutsch Collection, CORBIS; p62 *Granite Islands, River Nile* © Christine Osborne, CORBIS; p65 *Detail of Roman Gladiator Mosaic from Torre Nuova* © Alinari Archives, CORBIS; p69 *Napoleon's Troops Retreating from Moscow* (1888–89) by Jan van Chelminski © Agra Art, Warsaw, Poland, Bridgeman Art Library; p70 *The Aurora Borealis* © Lehtikuva Oy, REX FEATURES; p74 *Yuri Gagarin* © Bettmann, CORBIS; p76 *Tourist at the Santa Cruz Mystery Spot* © James A. Sugar, CORBIS; p81 *Mandela Speaking in Stadium After Release* © Peter Turnley, CORBIS; p90 *Air Force One* © bfi Collections; p90 *99 Things to do Before You Die* © Princess Productions; p93 *Taung Child Fossil* © Pascal Goetgheluck, Science Photo Library; p94 *Green Violet-Ear Bird Feeding at an Orchid* © Michael and Patricia Fogden, CORBIS; p95 *Machu Picchu*, Photodisk; p95 *Cave Paintings* © Sipa Press, REX FEATURES; p100 *Two Girls Reading* © John Walmsley; p108 *Donald Pleasance in You Only Live Twice* © bfi Collections; p118 *Irish Wheel Car* © Sean Sexton Collection, CORBIS; p120 *Star Wars* © LucasFilm, 20th Century Fox, The Kobal Collection; p121 *Interior of Lucullus Antique Store* © Robert Holmes, CORBIS.

Copyright illustrations:

pp6, 38, 45–46 and 66 © Mark Turner, 2004, Beehive Illustration; p27 © Colin Brown, 2004, Beehive Illustration; ; pp51 and 82 © Geoff Jones, 2004, Beehive Illustration; p76 © Martin Sanders, 2004, Beehive Illustration; p112 © Alan Down, 2004, Beehive Illustration.

Every effort has been made to trace copyright holders of material reproduced in this book. Any rights not acknowledged here will be acknowledged in subsequent printings if notice is given to the publisher.